Praise for *Victory is in the Struggle*

"An intense, captivating look at one of the most important human rights activists and scholars of the 20th century, Victory is in the Struggle is brave and challenging. In a moment when we need our elder voices to share how to struggle, Carlos Muñoz leaves us with this regalo. May we all have the audacity to ignite matches of justice and liberation that Muñoz leaves us with."
—**Pablo Gonzalez**, Continuing Lecturer Chicanx and Latinx Studies Program UC Berkeley

"Carlos Muñoz, Jr.'s memoir, *Victory is in the Struggle*, is the simple story of a remarkable man whose commitment to social justice, courage, and compassion are rooted in a life of overcoming poverty and racial injustice and helping others to do so as well. A Chicano Movement leader and cofounder of its student and scholarly organizations and of the first Chicano Studies Department in the country, and its first acting chair, Carlos's life is a list of meaningful firsts. This is the moving, inspiring, and historically significant life of a man of integrity."
—**Laura E. Pérez**, Professor of the Chicanx Latinx Studies Program and the Department of Ethnic Studies, University of California, Berkeley

"Carlos Muñoz has given us a concise first-hand account of the leaders, events, and organizations that comprised the movement for Chicano(a) identity, justice, and equality. His moving personal story of overcoming poverty and a lack of support from his parents to rise to the heights of academic achievement should inspire all who read it."

—**Charles Henry,** Professor Emeritus of African American Studies, UC-Berkeley

"Carlos Muñoz's compelling political memoir brilliantly illuminates a remarkable personal journey within the long, complex, and enduring Chicano Freedom Struggle. At the same time, this deeply moving work insightfully explores the broader historical significance and impact of this essential human rights struggle. A must read!"

—**Waldo E. Martin, Jr. Alexander F. and May T. Morrison** Professor of American History and Citizenship, Department of History. UC Berkeley

"*Victory is in the Struggle* is an intimate look at the life of a veteran of the Chicano Movement, a pioneering Ethnic Studies scholar, and a true organic intellectual, Carlos Muñoz Jr's commitment to building an «authentic revolutionary multiracial democracy» were shaped by war—his grandfather's involvement in Pancho Villa's revolutionary army, his experiences conducting military intelligence during the Korean War, which opened his eyes to violent machinations of U.S. imperialism, and his work as a scholar and activist challenging "internal colonialism" in Chicano communities. As "Profe" would often remind his students, "victory is in the struggle!"

—**Michael Schulze-Oechtering Castañeda**. Assistant Professor of History, California State University, East Bay

"In this important book, Muñoz takes us on a tour de force journey into his life of struggle and social movement activism. *Victory in the Struggle* beautifully captures the lived experience of revolutionary movements of the 1960s, the challenges of collective action, and the beauty of a life dedicated to the service of others. Most importantly, Muñoz pays special attention to the social relationships of love and solidarity built through a life of struggle. Gripping, emotional, and historically rich, this is a story that everyone needs to know."

—**Juan Herrera,** PhD. Associate Professor of Geography, University of California, Los Angeles

VICTORY IS IN THE STRUGGLE

FROM BARRIO BOY TO REVOLUTIONARY & SCHOLAR

DR. CARLOS MUÑOZ JR.

Eastwind Books of Berkeley

Victory Is in The Struggle
From Barrio Boy to Revolutionary & Scholar

Copyright © 2023 by Carlos Muñoz Jr

Published by:
Berkeley, California USA
www.AsiaBookCenter.com
email: eastwindbooks@gmail.com

Cover Design: Abraham Ramirez

All rights reserved. No part of this book may be used or reproduced without written permission from the author and publisher.

Eastwind Books of Berkeley is a registered trademark of Eastwind Books of Berkeley

Published 2023. First Edition
Printed in the United States of America

ISBN: 9781734744095 (Paperback)
ISBN: 9781961562042 (Ebook)

10 9 8 7 6 5 4 3 2 1

Dedication

I dedicate this book to my wife Chela, our two children: Daniel (Meghan) and Marcelo (Cynthia). And to my other children: Carlos, Marina (Ron), and Genaro (Keisha). And to my grandchildren in order of age: Esperanza (Jake), Emaney, Chloe, Sydni, Amaya, Joshua, Quetzally, Hailee, Rowan, Aeden, Marcelito Calixto, and Gabriella Concepciõn.

My wife Graciela Eulalia Rios Muñoz, "Chela", has been a major blessing. At this writing, we have been married 45 years. Without her I would not have known love and true happiness. She means the world to me. She has been a comrade in the struggle for racial and social justice. She is a true Woman Warrior who has made a difference in people's lives, especially during the time she worked as a social worker amongst the poor. She helped many people survive in this cruel capitalist society.

Acknowledgements

I thank my colleagues who have been supportive throughout my teaching and writing career. And to those who became comrades in the struggles for justice from all forms of oppression. Especially Dr. Mario Barrera and the late Dr. Danny Moreno. Special thanks to Dr. Harvey Dong and Dr. Pablo Gonzalez for their help and support in the publication of the book. And to the thousands of students that I was blessed to teach, especially to the hundreds that became activists and involved with efforts to change this country and the world for the better.

Contents

Dedication .... *vii*

Acknowledgements .... *ix*

Introduction .... *xiii*

Foreward .... *xv*

CHAPTER 1 Family History 1

CHAPTER 2 Barrio Boy 7

CHAPTER 3 From Barrio Boy to Soldier 31

CHAPTER 4 Becoming a Student Activist:
East LA Walkouts 43

CHAPTER 5 The Struggle for Chicano/a & Ethnic Studies
in the Academy 65

CHAPTER 6 Conclusion 89

Author Biography *103*

Introduction

I became a political prisoner in 1968 and faced a sentence of 66 years in prison for the "crime" of organizing high school student protest against racism in the East Los Angeles public schools. This experience contributed to my decision to write this book so that the story can be an inspiration to continue the struggle against racism and all forms of oppression; and make possible, justice for all. I am grateful for the 1st Amendment to the U.S. Constitution that gave me the freedom of speech to organize and speak out against racial injustice.

This book is a product of my journey through life. It's been an extremely long one. Full of joy as well as sadness. Joyful because I have been blessed with the opportunity to make a difference in people's lives. Sadness because I have lost family, and many good friends and comrades to the spirit world. Regretfully, my father, Carlos Garcia Muñoz and mother Clementina Contreras, joined the spirit world and were not alive to witness my blessings. My stepmother Consuelo Diaz who raised me also joined the spirit world. But I know they are smiling wherever they are.

Foreword

By Dr. Gabriela Spears-Rico

Carlos Muñoz Jr.'s contributions are embedded in every major significant event in the contemporary history of Chicana/os in the United States. Carlos is generous with his storytelling and trusts his readers. This deeply personal memoir not only offers a rare glimpse into the vulnerabilities, struggles, and courageous *espiritu* of a man, but also critically engages with the current debates that are evolving within Leftist activism and in the field of Chicana/o/x Studies. From Latina/o intersectionality to building multiracial coalitions to dealing with class divisions and addressing intra-group inequalities, his life and scholarship deal with the difficult questions of what it takes to get free. *Victory is in the Struggle* is moving, powerful and beautiful because it shows us a bare portrait of a Chicano scholar in ways we have not read before: Carlos reveals his battle wounds and scars to demonstrate the spirit of tenacity that emerges when a person lives a life dedicated to their values and, in doing so, this memoir debunks stereotypes that still portray Chicano male activists through a one-dimensional frame. Carlos risked so much in the fights to found Chicana/o and Ethnic Studies and became one of the discipline's most influential thinkers. His life, his rise out of neglect and poverty, his barrio truths, his commitment to racial and economic justice and to Chicano liberation are truly inspirational. With all he gave to the movimiento, Carlos resisted becoming a martyr. Instead, he kept his feet on the ground even as he became a well-respected academic. He continued to organize and stay grounded. This book shows us how his belief that victory is in the struggle inspired his desire to not give up on what is worth fighting for. His life as a veteran, as a citizen, as an academic and as an activist, models scholar-activism. This will be an impactful book in our field and in chronicling the history of Latinos in the United States. There are important lessons in this book. I hope our young people read him and are listening.

—**Dr. Gabriela Spears-Rico, Ph.D.,** McKnight Land-Grant Assistant Professor of Chicano Latino Studies, University of Minnesota Twin Cities

Chapter 1

Family History

Left: Grandfather Calixto Contreras (1897). Right: General Calixto Contreras is seated in bottom row, third from left. (*Photo credit: Museo a la Revolución, Mexico City*)

My parents were Carlos Garcia Muñiz and Clementina Contreras. They were born during the 1910 Mexican Revolution, the most violent revolution at that time in world history. It was followed by the 1917 Russian Revolution.

My paternal grandparents, Julio Muñiz and Maria Garcia, lived in the Valle de Allende, a small silver mining town in the state of Chihuahua, Mexico. It was one of the areas where Pancho Villa regularly visited to recruit young men for his revolutionary army and gather food supplies from the townspeople. Some of them gave the food voluntarily and others did not. My relatives whose food was taken consequently had negative feelings toward the revolution.

My Muñiz family therefore did not join the revolution but also did not support the dictatorship. My father was born in 1914 and he was the youngest of four children. His brother Jose was the older of the four. His sister Maria was the next oldest, followed by brother Edwardo. My grandmother died when my father was very young.

After her death, my grandfather feared the children would become victims of the revolutionary violence surrounding the area where they lived. So, he sent the three oldest siblings to live with relatives in Juarez, Mexico, and my father to live with a distant relative in El Paso, Texas, across the border from Juarez, Mexico. His name was Jose Guevara. I came to know him as "papa Pepe" and his wife Antonia as "mama Toña". That's what my father called them because they raised him since he arrived as a child refugee from the Revolution.

My Contreras family lived in Cuencame, Durango, Mexico, where my mother was born in 1916. It was a largely rural area next to the state of Chihuahua. It was also a silver mining area but in addition it was known for its agriculture. The area of Cuencame became a historic site of much of the early organizing against the Dictatorship of President Porfirio Diaz. In contrast to my Muñiz family, all the Contreras family joined the revolution. As a matter of fact, my maternal grandfather, Calixto Contreras, became a prominent leader of one of the first uprisings against the Diaz Dictatorship prior to the start of the

1910 revolution. He was known to both friends and enemies as "el Indio".

In 1897, my grandfather started defending the land holdings of his and other indigenous people against the efforts of big Mexican landowners and U.S. corporations to take over their lands. The loss of their land contributed to their bankruptcy and descent into poverty. In 1901 he and 17 members of his extended Contreras family signed an open letter which they sent to the Dictator President Porfirio Diaz requesting his intervention to protect their land rights. When he refused to do so, Calixto organized direct nonviolent protest actions against Diaz.

In 1905, he was arrested for protesting and agitating against the President. As was the case with those who opposed the Dictatorship, he was sentenced to mandatory military service in the Dictatorship's army. During that time, he learned much about weaponry and military tactics.

After he served his term of forced military service, he organized an armed brigade. The members of the brigade were from his family and the other indigenous families in the Cuencame area of Durango whose lands had been stolen. Calixto named his brigade "Benito Juarez" in honor of the first full blooded indigenous Mexican president who fought the French when they invaded Mexico on May 5, 1886. That date became a Mexican holiday named "Cinco de Mayo" to commemorate the war against France.

Calixto led his Juarez Brigade to war against the dictatorship. He subsequently joined Pancho Villa's Revolutionary

Northern Division Army and became one of Villa's generals. His Juarez Brigade became one of the bravest brigades of Villa's army.

Villa sent him and another of his leading generals, Felipe Angeles, to meet with Emiliano Zapata to forge an alliance between his Northern Division and Zapata's Southern Division army. Zapata had been reluctant to join forces because Villa had not originally made land reform a central part of his agenda. But Zapata had much respect for my grandfather because he had led the armed struggle against the Dictatorship in Durango prior to the start of the 1910 revolution. When they met, Zapata told him he was honored to meet him because of his "legendary role" in the struggle to return the land to his indigenous people in Durango.

The Alliance between Zapata's and Villa's forces that my grandfather and his comrade Felipe Angeles forged resulted in the defeat of the Diaz Dictatorship. After their victory, Zapata and Villa discussed which of them should become the new provisional President. Neither man wanted the job. Villa recommended Felipe Angeles, a graduate of Mexico's "West Point", to replace Diaz as president because he was the only one of his generals who was well educated. But Zapata wanted Calixto to become the president. Villa was surprised and responded that he had the highest regard for my grandfather but that he was not as educated as General Angeles. Zapata, however, argued that he "preferred Calixto because he knew that he would never betray the revolution". This was indeed high praise for my grandfather.

Generals who led other revolutionary groups also wanted

to be president and they engaged in a power struggle with Villa and Zapata. One of those was General Venustiano Carranza, the leader of the revolutionary "Constitutional Army". In 1916 During their internal struggle, U.S. troops were sent into Mexico in pursuit of Pancho Villa. My grandfather called it a direct invasion of Mexico. He argued that internal struggles should stop to forge an alliance of the various revolutionary groups to fight the "Yankee" invasion.

On the way to a meeting with the various generals where that unity could be forged, my grandfather was assassinated by one of Carranza's officers. Three years later, in 1919, Carranza also had Zapata assassinated. Their assassinations opened the way for Carranza to become the first revolutionary President of Mexico. Villa was assassinated after Carranza became president to assure Villa would not undermine his presidency.

NORTH FROM MEXICO

My mother was born the same year my grandfather was assassinated. Like my father, she arrived in El Paso as a child refugee. She was only 2 years old when she and her mother, Maria de Jesus Chávez de Garduño, crossed the US-Mexico border. My father was born in 1914 and was a couple years older when relatives crossed him over the border. My mother ended up in a Catholic orphanage and my father was lucky to end up with a relative in El Paso.

My parents were part of the waves of Mexican refugees, approximately 1 million of them, who arrived in El Paso during the Mexican Revolution. About another million Mexicans died during the revolution. At that time, it was the most violent revolution the world had ever known until the 1917 Russian Revolution.

The refugees were not met with open arms by the majority of white Americans. During the time they arrived signs were posted at stores, restaurants and public places that read "No dogs, no Negroes, no Mexicans". Prior to the arrival of most Mexican refugees and during the time of their arrival, Mexican Americans faced constant attacks by the Texas Rangers who were the most prominent law enforcement agency in Texas and patrolled the Mexico-U.S. border. They perceived Mexican male refugees as thieves and criminals. They killed many of them, either with weapons or by hanging them. Many were falsely accused of committing crimes. The Rangers had the racist mentally that the only good Mexican was a dead one. Mexican refugees confronted the same racist reality that Mexican Americans had experienced historically in the USA since the end of the U.S.-Mexico War of 1846-48 that resulted with Mexico's loss of approximately half of its territory.

Chapter 2

Barrio Boy

Carlos Muñoz Jr. Age 12. Photo right: El Segundo Barrio, El Paso, Texas

If I had been born in Mexico, my birth name would have been Carlos Luis Muñiz Contreras. My mother's last name was Contreras, and in Mexico the mother's last name comes after the father's last name. Unfortunately, my father's last name was changed from Muñiz to Muñoz when he became a naturalized citizen.

My father's legal name became Carlos Garcia Muñoz. The name change took place before my father was naturalized, when he was in elementary school in El Paso. The white teacher had never seen the name Muñiz and assumed that it was a typo, a misspelling of the name Muñoz, which she did know. She therefore had the school change the name on his records to Muñoz. The relatives who were taking care of him did not bother to have it changed back to Muñiz, and neither did he after becoming a citizen. When I was born, therefore, I was given the name of Carlos Muñoz, Jr., rather than Muñiz and without the Contreras from my mother's family.

I was born in the segregated Segundo Barrio in the city of El Paso on August 25, 1939. The dark clouds of World War II were on the horizon, with Adolf Hitler's army invading Poland a week after I was born. As I was growing up, the war became real to me via Hollywood war movies and the newsreels about the real war that were common in movie theaters during that time. Like many other kids, I remember enjoying playing with toy soldiers.

When I was in the fifth grade, my white teacher asked me where I was born. I answered, "Here, ma'am—in El Paso." She then replied, "So you're an American, not a Mexican! Your name should be Charles." I have never forgotten the day this happened. It was during the month of May 1951, the day General Douglas MacArthur, a World War II hero, spoke to the U.S. Congress after being dismissed by President Truman as the commanding general of the U.S. forces in Asia. Our teacher turned on the radio so the class could listen to his speech. His closing words have always stayed with me: "Old soldiers never die; they just fade away." I shed some tears. My teacher was touched when I cried. She was convinced I was proud to be an American, and she had the school formally change my first name to Charles. I remember running home and telling my father, "Apa, my name is now Char-less!" He replied, "OK, m'ijo, but never forget here at home you are Carlos!" Other kids, including my cousins across the border in Juárez, started calling me "Charlie," and that name stayed with me from that time until I changed my name back to Carlos after my honorable discharge from the U.S. Army in 1962.

My mother never knew this happened to me because she died of tuberculosis when I was three years old. As was the case with people with TB at the time, she was isolated because TB is an infectious disease and there was still no cure. Therefore, she could not stay near me, and instead she stayed in the house where my father had been raised by the relatives, Pepe and Toña Guevara. She was isolated in a small upstairs room, and my father would take me to visit her and I would play outside the house from where she could see me from her upstairs room window and she would wave at me. I would wave back, but I could not see her very well.

My father suffered a nervous breakdown after my mother's death and turned to alcohol to deal with his emotional pain. He became an alcoholic and could not take care of me. Relatives did not want to take care of me because they assumed my mother had passed the TB to me and they were afraid they might catch it. The Guevaras took care of me until my father's older brother José, who was called "Che," and his wife, Lela, took me in when I turned four years old. But they made clear that the arrangement was only temporary until my father remarried. I lived with them in a one-room apartment in a run-down two-story tenement building without a bathroom. Everyone in that building had to use a "community" wooden toilet located outside at the end of each floor of the building.

One day I was playing "hide and seek" with other kids and I had to urinate, so I went into the toilet. Then someone else, not another kid, went in after me and told me to bend down because it was part of the game. I then felt something hard penetrate my behind. It hurt and I cried. I did not know I was being raped. I still remember waking up to nightmares and crying loudly in the middle of the night for many days afterwards. I never told anyone what had happened to me.

The tenement building was located in the small "Chihuahuito Barrio," which was next to the larger Segundo Barrio, where I had been born, and a stone's throw away from the U.S.–Mexico border. The Oregon Street bridge that crossed the Rio Grande and connected El Paso with Juárez, Mexico, was about a block away. The Stanton Street Bridge that connected Juárez with El Paso was another few blocks away at the edge of the Segundo Barrio. A streetcar would go from downtown El Paso on Stanton Street cross the bridge and continue into downtown Juárez and return on Oregon Street. I loved riding that streetcar when I went to play with my Muñiz cousins in the working-class Juárez barrio called "La Chaveña."

When World War II was in full swing my father tried to join the U.S. Army, not because of any patriotic impulse, but in the hope of getting killed on the battlefield. That was the only way he thought he could deal with the loss of my mother. But he was rejected as 4F, "unfit for military duty," due to the nervous breakdown he suffered after my mother died. Eventually, he was able to get a job building warships in Vancouver, Canada. He then remarried so I could have a mother to take care of me. I did not know until I was an adult that she was only sixteen years old at the time. She was the niece of the husband of my father's sister, Maria. They lived in Juárez, Mexico. Her name was Consuelo Diaz but was known as "Chelo." My father took her to El Paso without any problem because she had a U.S. citizen passport. The passport belonged to a sister by the name of Guadalupe, who had been born in El Paso during the time her father came to the U.S. to work in the building of the U.S. railroad. The sister died, and Chelo was given her passport after she married my father. All her life in the U.S. she used her dead sister's name of Guadalupe in order to pass as a U.S. citizen. She never learned how to speak English and relied on my father and me to be her interpreters. She never worked because she always feared that la migra, as immigration officials were called, would discover that her name was not Guadalupe.

Unfortunately, Chelo was not a good stepmother to me. She was too young to know how to be a mother when she married my father. She became frustrated with my father's drinking and felt burdened by me. Plus, she could not have her own children. She took out her frustrations on me with physical and emotional violence. The only times she was nice to me and showed affection was in the company of friends or strangers. I never felt loved by her. As soon as school was out for the summer, she would take me to live with her family in Mexico so that she could get rid of me.

Fortunately, that turned out to be a blessing. The family welcomed me with open arms and gave me the love and attention

I never got from Chelo or my father back home in the U.S. They all called me "Carlitos," the affectionate name for Carlos. I have fond memories of her father, José Diaz, whom I grew to love as my abuelito (grandfather). He would intervene on my behalf when I was hit or yelled at by my stepmother. Chelo's seven siblings, whom I came to love as tías and tíos (aunts and uncles) also defended me from Chelo's anger. Summers in Mexico were full of love and adventure with Chelo's family. Her father worked for the Mexican railroad as an train engineer, and every few years he would be transferred to a different city and would take his family with him. I got to know several Mexican cities when living with them during the summers until I was about fifteen years old.

A benefit of my abuelito's employment was free train travel for all the members of his family. I got to travel free by using the name of "Filimon," one of Chelo's brothers who had died as a child. So I was called "Filimon" when traveling in Mexico on the train to get free passage. In addition to living in Gómez Palacio for a year after my father's marriage to Chelo, I later had the opportunity to spend summers in the cities of Aguascalientes, Nuevo Laredo, and Juárez.

Gómez Palacio, Durango, was the most memorable for me because it was close to where my mother, Clementina, was born and because it was the first time I lived with Chelo's family. It was for a whole year. I was five years old at the time and I attended kindergarten at the local elementary school where Chelo's brother Agustine worked as a janitor. The name of the school was "16 de Marzo" in honor of the birthday of one of Mexico's legendary heroes, Benito Juárez. I remember the family bought me a charro outfit so I could participate in a school festival. I danced the Jarabe Tapatío, one of the most popular Mexican dances.

Chelo's family knew about my maternal grandfather Calixto Contreras and the role he played in making the 1910 Revolution in the state of Durango and elsewhere. They told me that he was the general who led one of the early battles of the 1910 Revolution that was fought near Gómez Palacio.

I had many memorable adventures hanging out with my tíos. One of the most memorable, and the scariest, was during one summer in Juarez, Mexico, after the family moved when abuelito José Diaz retired from the railroad. I was then about eleven years old. My youngest tío, Armando, was about seventeen and wanted very much to become a bullfighter. He would take me to the Plaza de Toros in Juárez to check out the bulls in the fenced yards behind the bull ring where they kept them. He made me walk right behind him on top of the narrow concrete fence, being very careful not to lose my balance for fear of falling into the yards with the bulls. When there was a bullfight, he would sneak us in behind the bleacher seats to see it. He never became a bullfighter, but did become a picador, the one who rode a horse and would poke the bull with a lance to get it away from the bullfighter if it appeared he was close to being gored. Pepe was another brother of Chelo, whose company I enjoyed. He introduced me to the game of baseball. He had played professional baseball at the Mexican minor league level, and he would take me to professional baseball games. He gave me my first baseball glove, which I kept for many years.

I also enjoyed being with Ernesto, the husband of Chelo's sister Lola. He was an umpire in the Mexican major leagues in the city of Aquascalientes, where I spent one summer. He would take me to the baseball games he umpired. He was the darkest of the family and could pass for an African American back home in the States. I asked tia Lola why he was darker than the rest of us and she told me she thought it was maybe because he had a Cuban grandfather. At that time, it was not generally known that the Spaniards brought African slaves to Mexico after the conquest in 1521. It was not until the beginning of the twentieth century that the Mexican government acknowledged that the third root of Mexican culture was African.

The first book to document the presence of African Mexicans was published in 1947. Since then, others have been published by Mexican scholars documenting the history of slavery in Mexico and the continued existence of African Mexicans. They are mostly visible in the states of Veracruz, Guerrero, and Oaxaca, although they live in many areas throughout Mexico. Unfortunately, however, the majority of my family believed, as did most Mexicans, that their culture is rooted only in Indigenous and Spanish cultures. I didn't really discover African Mexicans, or Afro Mestizos, as they have become known, until I visited Veracruz in 1976 when I was in my mid-thirties.

Living with Chelo's family during the summers until the age of fifteen contributed to my appreciation and love of working-class Mexican culture and their way of life. Thanks to them, I grew to know Mexico and take an interest in Mexican history.

THE SEGUNDO BARRIO

Back home in the USA and growing up in El Paso's Segundo Barrio was like living in another world, a world without the love and affection I experienced in Mexico. My father had learned how to do carpentry during his youth, and he became real good at it. He had to deal with racism on the construction jobs he had, racist discrimination that resulted in low wages. Consequently, he often had trouble paying our rent on time, and we therefore got evicted often from places where we lived. The place where we lived the longest was a one-room tenement apartment on 5th and Campbell Streets in the Segundo Barrio. I also remember living in a cheap hotel room when I was about nine years old in downtown El Paso that was near my Guevara relatives. I liked it because it was about a block away from the downtown Alligator Plaza and across the street from the Crawford movie theater. There was no bathroom in the room, so we had to share the hotel bath and toilet. I would sleep at the feet of my parents on the same bed.

An elderly white hotel tenant would invite me to have a can of Campbell's soup in his room when I was hungry. Living in the hotel is where I first saw dead people. I had gone to the room where a playmate lived. While knocking on the door I smelled gas and no one answered. I ran to get the hotel manager and when he opened the door, I saw my friend, his sister, and their parents dead on the floor. They had died from the gas poisoning. Another place I remember was sharing a house with a friend of my father's. Our living space was the dining room with one bed and a chest of drawers. I would sleep on the floor.

Growing up, food was not plentiful. My diet largely

consisted of beans, rice, and tortillas. I started working at the age of six to help put food on the table. After school my stepmother would send me to do errands and odd jobs for people. When the soles of my shoes got holes in them, she would put cardboard in my shoes to cover them up. The job I liked the most was selling the El Paso Times newspaper at nearby Fort Bliss every Sunday when I was about ten years old. The newspaper truck would pick up me and the other kids early in the morning at the downtown public library. The soldiers would give us good tips and best of all, the cooks would give us free meals—it was the first time I had steak. I never imagined that one day I would also be a soldier stationed on that Army base.

I have one good memory of my stepmother. She would occasionally take me to the Colón movie theater, located in the Segundo Barrio, a theater that featured Mexican movies. I enjoyed watching those movies, especially the ones about the 1910 Revolution. My favorite actors were Pedro Armendáriz, Jorge Negrete, Pedro Infante, María Félix and Dolores Del Rio, as well as the Mexican comedian Cantinflas, who filled me with laughter.

On the home front, it was different from attending Mexican movies with Chelo. I enjoyed her company at the movies, but not at home. She and my father would argue when he was drunk, but he never hit her. She, on the other hand, would hit him. I'll never forget how one time she beat him up with a steel frying pan when he was drunk.

On some weekends, my parents would take off to party in the bars in Juárez. I would have to hang around outside the bars, or they would leave me at home—which I preferred because my father would give me a dollar to go to the movies. Admission was only ten cents, and I would go to all the downtown theaters watching American movies all day. Movies became my favorite pastime, helping me escape the harsh realities I had to put up with at home and the insecurity of walking the city streets at night alone.

Unfortunately, most of my memories of my stepmother are bad ones. I still vividly remember being knocked out at the breakfast table when she hit me with a coffee cup because I did not want to eat my breakfast. Another one was when I came home from school with a deep cut on my chin that occurred when I fell off a small cliff near the school, where I was playing with a friend. I got home with blood covering the front of my white shirt. Instead of comforting me, she angrily grabbed a broom and started beating me up with the wood part of the broom because I had dirtied the white shirt. In addition to physical violence, I had to put up with emotional violence that was manifested in loud screams anytime she thought I did something wrong. She constantly would tell me I could not do anything right. After becoming a teenager, we got along better because she stopped hitting me. But she continued yelling at me.

Living in the Segundo Barrio exposed me to gangs. I lived several blocks away from the segregated Bowie High School and the area from there to my house was the territory of the 7-X gang. I knew that because their graffiti were all over the place. I did get to know some gang members during the day when they would play touch football on the street around the corner from where I lived. Most of them were teenagers and they seemed to be good guys, but I never became friends with any of them. I never lived long enough in one place to make friends. I made only one good friend at school, but he did not live near me. He lived across Paisano Drive, the dividing line between El Segundo Barrio and downtown El Paso. His name was Santiago Wong. His father was Chinese, and his mother was Mexican, and they owned a Chinese restaurant. We would walk to and from school together. Usually, his parents would invite me to eat in their restaurant. I loved their Chinese food! Hanging out with Santiago resulted in other kids calling me el Chino, loosely translated as "the Chinese guy." Interestingly, I looked more Chinese than Santiago. I would get angry when other Chicano kids would sing a racist song to me that went, "Chino, Chino, Japones, come caca and no me des." Loosely translated it was, "Chinese, Chinese, Japanese, eat shit and don't give me any."

Not having close friends in the Segundo Barrio, I would walk across the border bridge to visit my Muñiz family in Juárez most weekends. I enjoyed playing and hanging out with my cousins, especially Ernesto, who was called "Neto." We were like brothers. When my stepmother's family moved to Juárez after the railroad transferred my abuelito there, I could visit them as well. So those were happy times for me and offered another escape from the problems I had to deal with at home and on the streets in El Segundo Barrio.

At that time, crossing the border was not a problem. The border guards were not armed and always friendly, at least to kids. When they asked what my citizenship was, I would answer, "Merican." Some of them would smile and allow me to pass. Years later during the Clinton presidency, the border became a militarized zone, and the border guards were armed and no longer friendly.

When I turned twelve years old in 1952, my father decided to move us to Los Angeles in search of a better life. We ended up living in East Los Angeles in the Boyle Heights Barrio. I came to know it as the "White Fence" barrio—the name of the gang that held "territorial rights" in that area. We arrived with no place to live, but luckily we did not become homeless because an elderly friend of someone my father knew allowed us to stay on the side porch of her house on Alma Street, near 1st Street, about a block away from where a mercado now stands. A screen and an aluminum roof enclosed the porch, and we had access to the kitchen and bathroom. I'll never forget walking into the kitchen one day to get a bite to eat and seeing the elderly lady on the floor. I thought she had fallen, but then I discovered that she was dead. We had to move out after her death.

We moved to a barrio in downtown LA called Bunker Hill. My father rented a cheap one room place in an old two-story Victorian house. It only had a hot plate to cook on, a bathroom, a piece of furniture for clothes, and a bed. I slept on the floor. The house was located in an alley named Clay Street that was about three blocks long and went under the tracks of a small cable car named "Angel's Flight" that took passengers from Hill Street downtown up to the top of Bunker Hill. The house faced the Grand Central Market, located below on Hill Street, which was mostly a Mexican mercado that included small restaurant-type spaces and is still located there. It was a convenient location for us to buy inexpensive groceries. I enjoyed living on Clay Street because it was a stone's throw from the Million Dollar movie theater on Broadway Street, which featured Mexican movies and live performances by popular Mexican singers and mariachis.

The house was also very close to the main Los Angeles Public Library, where I would go to get off the streets and hide out from gang conflicts. I soon fell in love with books. My favorites were the ones about sports heroes, especially New York Yankee baseball superstars like Babe Ruth and Lou Gehrig. I also hung out at nearby Pershing Square, where I would sit and watch dogs that people walked and dream about having a dog someday.

We then moved from Clay Street up to Olive Street at the top of Bunker Hill, a stone's throw away from the Los Angeles City Hall and the old City Jail. While living there I went to an elementary school to finish the sixth grade. One day a cop by the name of Sgt. Rivera went to the school to recruit kids for his Boy Scout troop. He spoke about going on camping trips to the Mojave Desert. It sounded like fun, so I joined up. It was my first experience camping and I loved it. Our weekly meetings were held in a cell in the nearby City Jail on First Street. He said that he had the meetings there so we could get the feel about being in jail, and thus motivate us to stay away from trouble. It worked for me, and I vowed never to do something that would put me in jail.

At night, when I could not stand being home due to loud arguments between my parents or being yelled at by my stepmother, I would take lonely walks all over the downtown streets checking out store windows to see what was on sale, although I did not have any money to shop. I would stop by movie theaters to check out the outside posters about the movies they were playing, and I would simply watch people-watch. When I walked the lonely streets at night, I would wish I was an orphan so I could live in an orphanage, someplace where I would be fed and live in peace.

I started attending John Adams Junior High School, a largely African American school with a visible minority of Mexican American kids. The school was located near the LA Coliseum, and I had to take the streetcar downtown to get there. If I did not have the money for the fare, I had to walk about two miles. I did not mind that, because I liked school and decided that school was going to be my safe haven from my dysfunctional family life and the unfriendly streets. I excelled academically and had fun playing sports on the school's playground. I was one of two Mexican American students who made the Honor Society. I was the only male student in that group that had a "ducktail" haircut and wore khaki pants, a white t-shirt, and a brown leather jacket, which was sort of the uniform of gang members or wannabe gang members. The other honor society members were mostly white or Asian; I don't recall any African Americans. I also joined the school glee club and sang baritone.

I was lucky to have a teacher who encouraged me to study and to play sports. His name was James Taylor, who was my math and homeroom teacher and the only African American teacher at the school. There were no Mexican American teachers, although there was a P.E. teacher whose last name was Galindo. He ignored me, so I did not get to know him like I did Mr. Taylor, who would always point me out in class as a positive example of a good student who kept out of trouble. He would invite me and other good students to his house to play basketball on his driveway basketball court and eat hamburgers he cooked on his outside grill.

Unfortunately, the only fights I had at school were with African American students. It was the first time in my life that I had attended school or interacted with Black kids. When they called me a motherfucker, I reacted in a fighting posture because those words translated into chinga tu madre in Spanish. Those were fighting words in Mexican culture because they dishonored mothers. I got to the point where I finally understood those bad words were only an expression and not a literal accusation among Black youth. And I got tired of engaging in fistfights.

After all the fights I was in, I thought about becoming a boxer because I kept being told I looked like Keeny Teran. He was a Mexican American boxer who was highly rated and named "Olympic Auditorium Fighter of the Year" when I started junior high school. I started going to the YMCA in Downtown LA to work out in the boxing gym. I liked hitting the punching bag because I could get all the anger out of me.

My last fight took place at a neighborhood playground when I was fifteen years old. A Black kid who was a friend of another Black kid I had beaten up badly in school took the basketball away from me in order to start a fight. We fought, but during the fight I thought, "Why am I doing this? Is a basketball worth it?" I stopped swinging and told the kid, "I don't want to fight anymore." I put my arms down and he hit me on the mouth. I wound up in the emergency room at the local hospital, where they sewed up my lip. (I still have the scar.) My plans to become a boxer ended at that hospital.

Up to that point in my life I was a loner; my only friends were at school, and most of them did not live near me. There was one, Joe Gandara, who did live on the same street as me. But he spent most of the time with his girlfriend. He was a member of the Olive Street gang, who would hang out across the street where I lived, and he invited me to join. For the first time I decided to become a "card-carrying" part of a gang. Gang members who I had known living in other LA barrios respected me because I was from El Paso, which had the fame of producing the "Pachuco" image of gang members. El Paso was known as "El Chuco." I took up the nickname of "Chino" and started doing graffiti on walls, signing off as "El Chino/EPT/CS." EPT was short for El Paso, Texas, and CS was short for Con Safos, which meant that whoever bad-mouthed me with a bad word, it rebounded back on them.

Our gang activity was largely hanging out on street corners, drinking cheap white port wine and beer. Most of the gang members smoked marijuana, though I stuck to the wine and beer and avoided the marijuana because it made me sleepy. We would walk through the barrio giving bad looks to other teenagers, especially if we thought they were members of another gang. We wanted to make sure they knew that the area was our territory. In those days, gang fights would usually involve fistfights, and occasionally a knife would be pulled. Gang life was not like it would become later, with fistfights tragically giving way to gunfights and killings. When cop cars approached us we tried hard to walk more macho. I discovered, however, that if

I stopped doing that and instead was polite to the cops who seemed bent on harassing me, they would stop—especially when I would tell them that I wanted to be a cop like them.

Like other kids who had dysfunctional families, I perceived the gang as "family" who would have my back. But I was wrong. "El Chuga," the gang leader, and I did not get along. One day he decided to take me on and started calling me puto (gay) to find out how much of a man I was. I came very close to losing my temper, clenching my fists and getting ready to defend myself. He called on other gang members to jump me—but none did, because I had their respect. I decided that it was braver for me to simply walk away hoping that they would not come after me. Luckily, they didn't. That experience of gang life left me with a sour taste, and I decided I had had enough violence in my life. I was tired of dealing with violence-prone situations, and I came to the conclusion that it was not right to fight each other, Mexican against Mexican. We were not each other's enemy, regardless of issues about whose gang territory was whose.

The LA Public Library and sports became my new way to pass the time, and I stopped hanging out in the street with the other guys. I found the library to be a peaceful and quiet place. I started liking to read again, especially biographies of athletes, in particular baseball players, but I also read biographies of nonathletes. I remember reading the biography of President Wilson, who was in office during World War I. I was impressed by him until I found out later as a college student that he ordered U.S. troops to invade Mexico in search of Pancho Villa. I also remember reading the autobiography of the famous lawyer Clarence Darrow, which was critical of the cops and prison system, and I gave thought to someday becoming a lawyer like him.

I went to the playgrounds and played basketball and baseball, and I dreamed about becoming a professional baseball player. During the baseball season I would take the streetcar all the way to Wrigley Field, the home of the Pacific Coast minor league Los Angeles Angels team. It cost me about a quarter to sit in the bleachers. I loved to watch my favorite player, Steve Bilko, the first baseman for the Angels, hit home runs and I would sit in the bleacher section where his home runs normally went—though unfortunately, I was never able to catch one.

In 1955, my first year in high school, the city planners decided Bunker Hill should undergo a massive slum clearance project. Property owners were bought out, and Mexican American and other poor renters were evicted. The area became home to the Los Angeles Music Center, upscale hotels, and corporate skyscrapers. We went through another eviction and moved to an apartment house several blocks from Belmont High School, on the outskirts of Bunker Hill, where I went to school. It was the largest place where we had ever lived up to then, with a bedroom, bathroom, kitchen, and a dining room area. For the first time in my life, I was able to have my own bed. It was in the corner next to the dining table. My father could afford the rent because he had joined Alcoholic Anonymous (AA), and he went sober for a couple of years, so he had and was able to keep a decent job.

Belmont High at that time happened to be the LA public high school where most of the immigrant kids were sent—it was therefore the most diverse high school in the city. My junior high school had been mostly African American, but at Belmont I got to know kids from other parts of the world, and I called it the "little United Nations" high school. In addition to Mexican and African Americans, U.S. white kids, and Hawaiians, my baseball and football teammates were also Asian. I had three best friends. They were Carl Smith, an African American; George Hirai, a Japanese American; and Roman Garcia, a Mexican American.

When I arrived for my freshman year, the academic adviser asked me what my father did for a living. I told her that he worked with his hands in construction. She told me that it was an "honorable profession and that I should follow in his footsteps." I did not know that at that time there was a vulgar tracking system: if you were an African or Mexican American male, you were assigned the Industrial Arts major, where you took wood shop and auto shop. I was therefore not given an Academic major, which was required for college admissions. The day she assigned me that major I went home happy to tell my father that I was told I should follow in his footsteps in terms of a job when I graduated. He got extremely upset and told me he did not want me to follow in his footsteps, because he wanted me to get a job working with a pencil and not a pick and shovel. The next day I met with the white academic adviser and told her, "My father does not want me to follow in his footsteps. He wants me to get a job working with a pencil." She thought about it for a minute and said, "Working with a pencil, eh? OK, I'll assign you a business major. You can then find a job as a used car salesman or bank clerk." I did not know that that major was one that was assigned only to girls (the other one was home economics). My first class was typing. When I walked in I was happy to see that the students were all girls. I was the only boy in the class, and I thought, "Hey, this is cool. I have all the cute girls to myself. I had no complaints about the major." I had no idea what was really going on, since I did not plan on going to college. My parents did not know about college—they just wanted me to finish high school. My father had only completed the fourth grade, and my stepmother the equivalent of elementary school in Mexico. The only positive about being a business major was learning how to type. That skill came in handy when I later served in the U.S. Army, where I became a clerk typist instead of fighting in the trenches, although I would have welcomed the opportunity to fight if I had to.

Although I was not assigned an Academic major, I made the academic honor societies because I got all A's and B's in general academic courses: English, government, history, and basic math, etc. I had no Mexican American teachers. My favorite class was government because I liked the teacher, Mrs. Hosack, who was white and handicapped. Her lectures were the most interesting. One day after class she called me over and asked me if my real name was Carlos and not Charles. I said yes, and she responded, "It's a beautiful name—you should start using it." No other adult had ever said that to me, not even Mexican Americans. I never forgot that moment, because she reminded me that I should be proud of who I was, and she also told me I had the makings of a good political leader.

In addition to academics, I also excelled in sports and made the varsity baseball and football teams. And, with the encouragement of Mrs. Hosack, I became a leader in student government and was elected class president in my junior year and student body president in my senior year. In 1957, when I served as junior class president, I played a role in making our school a sister school to Little Rock high school in Arkansas in support of the civil rights struggle to integrate that school. In 1958 as student body president, I made my first public speech at an educational conference, where I asked for support for integration of Black students in the South and Mexican Americans in the Southwest. The conference took place at the famous Los Angeles Coconut Grove Hotel, where presidential candidate Senator Robert F. Kennedy would be assassinated just ten years later.

To help out with home expenses and to get some spending money, I held different after-school and summer jobs during my junior high and senior high school years, though I had to make sure that those jobs did not interfere with my sports team practices after school. They included a newspaper route and working as a dishwasher at the downtown Woolworth's store on weekends, an apprentice house painter, and evenings at the U.S. Post Office in the summers and holiday seasons. My last part-time job was during high school at a lamp factory after school and Saturdays that employed formerly incarcerated Mexican and African Americans. I enjoyed working with them because they always treated me with respect. The manager was a white liberal guy and was always very nice to me and the other workers.

The factory was about a block from where I lived at that time, on Beaudry Street at the corner of 2nd Street. It was the territory of the Temple Street gang, arch enemies of the Alpine gang and the Olive Street gang, which I had been a member of during my junior high school days. I used to walk home from high school with a chain wrapped around my fist and carrying my books in my other hand. The chain was to make the Temple Street gang members that hung out near my home think twice about attacking me.

The only bad incident I confronted, however, did not involve that gang, but was courtesy of the LA police. When I worked at the lamp factory on Saturdays, I loved having a ham and egg breakfast at a small hole-in-the-wall restaurant across from the factory. (It was a real treat for me, because I never had ham and eggs at home.) One Saturday I was enjoying my breakfast when a squad car pulled up at the front of the restaurant and two cops walked in. One grabbed me from the arm and said, "Let's go!" He threw me into the car's back seat. I asked, "Where are you taking me?" His response was "Downtown—you fit the description of someone who committed a burglary." I assumed that they were taking me to jail, but the squad car stopped at an office building. One cop got out and went to the front entrance, where a white lady was standing. She nodded her head to indicate yes, then nodded to say no, and then she turned to the cop and said something. My anxiety level by that time was sky high—I feared I would be taken to jail for sure. The cop got into the squad car, turned to me and said, "You're a lucky Mexican—she said you were not the one." I was of course greatly relieved! I went back to work singing and whistling, and guys I worked with asked me why I was so happy.

I graduated with honors from Belmont High in June 1958 and made plans to attend community college to make up the academic courses I did not get the opportunity to take. After I would complete those courses, I planned to transfer to UCLA. I enrolled at East Los Angeles Community College in the fall of 1958. I was not assigned an academic counselor, and therefore I looked through the catalog and identified the courses I thought I should take. I chose an algebra class, thinking it was an introductory course. It was not—it was an advanced algebra class. Halfway through the semester I was getting a D and was on the verge of failing the class. Not having had an introductory course made it difficult for me to understand algebra. I had never received a grade below a B in high school, and I lost confidence in my academic ability. I thought it was perhaps true that Mexicans did not have the intellectual capacity to succeed in college due to their "culture of poverty." That was the racist image of my people that was promoted by both conservative and liberal white academics, by social workers, and in the mass media and Hollywood films. I dropped out of college.

Like other poor kids, I felt I did not have any viable options for a good job, so I decided to volunteer for the draft to get my military obligation over with, something that all men reaching the age of eighteen had at that time.

Chapter 3

From Barrio Boy to Soldier

US Army soldier, Carlos Muñoz Jr. was stationed in South Korea in 1961. Photo right: South Koreans protest General Park Chung-hee dictatorship in 1961 which the US supported for 30 years.

After I dropped out of East Los Angeles City College in 1959, I volunteered for the draft. At that time all young men who reached the age of 18 had to sign up for the draft to serve in the military. I wanted to get away and so did not want to wait until I was drafted. I was 20 years old. I was excited when I received my orders for the U.S. Army basic training at Fort Ord, California.

When I arrived with a bus load of other recruits, we were ordered to stand at attention and a sergeant barked out "those of you with prior military experience step forward!" There were several who had previously served in the air force, navy, or marines, and wanted for whatever reason to try the U.S. Army. Others had served in college ROTC. I asked the recruit next to me why they were being called out and he told me they would become squad leaders and a benefit of that was they would get their own private rooms and did not have to sleep in the dorms with the rest of us. That sounded good to me, so I stepped out. Each of those stepping out were asked what their previous military training or experience had been. When it came to my turn, I said "Boy Scouts Sir!". I had briefly been in the boy scouts in elementary school and remembered learning how to march and certain skills used in the military, e.g., setting up tents, how to use knifes, dig foxholes, and survive in the desert. So, I thought, hell, why not give it a try. The worst that could happen was that I would get a few laughs. The sergeants running the show looked at each other and smiled. I thought, here come the laughs! Instead, I was pleasantly shocked that I was told to move out with the others who had stepped forward. Then I was especially pleased when I was told I would become the platoon leader in charge of four squads. But those with real previous military service and who were not selected were not pleased. So, I expected that I would have to put up with them challenging my authority.

I was confident of my leadership skills. I had been a leader on the high school football and baseball teams. And I had been a leader in student government and served as Student Body President in my senior year. But I had to show I had no fear on the training battlefields and that I had the strength to succeed in the most arduous physical maneuvers and exercises. On one occasion leading my platoon back to the barracks on the sandy ground of the Monterey Bay from the rifle range I showed my leadership. One of the overweight recruits had a hard time running through the sand and fell several times. He weighed about 240 pounds. I picked him up and halfway carried him with his arm around my neck.

I maintained my stride leading the platoon and kept barking out the military cadence:

Sound-off; 1 - 2; Sound-off; 3 - 4
Cadence count; 1 - 2 - 3 - 4; 1 - 2 - 3 - 4

This action really impressed my platoon and gained me much respect.

During physical training sessions of the entire Brigade, I would be one of the leaders on the high platforms displaying how to correctly do the exercises, from jumping jacks to pull ups, etc. During battlefield maneuvers, I was selected to act as the "general" in charge of calling out the military tactics to be used. At the end of basic training, I was selected as the "Outstanding Trainee" of Company C, 9th Battle Group, 3rd Brigade. The officers and sergeants of our regiment encouraged me to apply to Officer Candidate School and make the Army my career. I seriously considered it. I had become a "gung-ho" soldier and started thinking about maybe becoming a general and following in the footsteps of my maternal grandfather Calixto's footsteps who had been a general in the 1910 Mexican Revolution.

I scored high in the aptitude test given in basic training and given my leadership success; I was assigned to the U.S. Army Information School at Fort Slocum in New York instead of Fort Benning in Georgia for Advanced Infantry training where the majority of the other recruits were sent. They flew me to New York City. It was my first airplane flight and although I was a bit nervous, I very much enjoyed it. Especially exciting was landing at the JFK airport and taking a bus through the famous big city to the location where I caught the subway train to the city of New Rochelle near Fort Slocum at the western end of Long Island Sound where the Army Information School was located. It could only be reached by ferry because the Fort was in the middle of large body of water.

I spent the winter of 1959 at Fort Slocum and had my first experience shoveling snow. I made two good friends. One of them was Joe Hubbard, Jr., an African American from South Los Angeles, and Jerry West a white Southerner from North or South Carolina. Joe loved Jazz and R & B music and Jerry loved the theater. We had the weekends off and we would catch the subway train to New York City to enjoy jazz in the famous nightclubs in Greenwich Village and Broadway shows at the theaters near Times Square. One of the most memorable music experiences I had was listening to Count Basie and his great Orchestra and the lovely voice of Joe Williams. It was my first introduction to Jazz. I also enjoyed the theater plays on Broadway that we saw. Especially the famous operatic play "Porgy and Bess" by playwright George Gershwin which featured an all-African American cast. One of the songs featured in the play was "Summertime". It has remained one of my favorite songs.

I very much enjoyed New York City and apart from the music and theater, I visited some of its fine museums, and walked through lovely grand central park. Plus, I enjoyed taking in a baseball game at Yankee Stadium. And for the first time in my life, I had the first opportunity to get to know Puerto Ricans. They welcomed me as a "brother". I found it interesting to hear them speak Spanish that was different from the way Mexicans spoke it. They called me "Calo" instead of Carlos, not pronouncing the "r" and "s" in my name. I enjoyed visiting Spanish Harlem and taking in the salsa music at bars and restaurants.

The US Army Information School was an interesting and enjoyable experience. It was like being in college. We were trained to be Public Affairs staff for the U.S. Army. We were taught the basics of print and media journalism for work in radio and television. We also received a heavy dose of anti-communist propaganda that we were expected to use to provide political indoctrination to the troops. I learned all about the "evils" of Communism that were espoused by Karl Marx, Lenin, and Trotsky. I later got different perspectives of those revolutionaries after my military service when I studied their works in college. Fort Slocum was shut down several years after I graduated from the Information School. The school evolved into a new U.S. Defense Information School at a new location and included all the branches of the military.

After all the training I received as a Public Affairs Information Specialist, I was disappointed to receive orders to report to the G2 (Army Intelligence) section at Fort Bliss, Texas, as a clerk typist and not as an "Information Specialist" that I was trained to be. But I did not complain because I was extremely happy to wind up at a place I got to know well when I was a kid. The Fort was located on the outskirts of my hometown of El Paso, Texas. When I was about 9 years old, I had a job selling the Sunday edition of the El Paso Times to the soldiers at Fort Bliss. I and other kids were picked up early in the morning at the downtown public library by the newspaper trucks. The few dollars I made helped my parents pay the rent or buy groceries. I enjoyed the job because the friendly Army cooks would invite me to eat free breakfast and lunch in their kitchens. The menu usually included steaks or fried chicken, and other foods I never ate at home. It was a much more exciting menu compared to the rice and beans I was used to eating daily.

I liked the G2 job because part of my duties included being a translator of Mexican newspaper articles that were deemed worthy of intelligence information. But most importantly, I liked it because being stationed there was like a dream come true. I was able to reconnect to my father's Muñiz family living in El Paso's Segundo Barrio where I was born and across the Rio Grande in Juárez, Mexico, in that city's "La Chaveña" working class barrio where some of my father's family lived. I had not seen them since I was 12 years old when I moved to East Los Angeles with my father and stepmother. I was able to visit them regularly and hang with my cousin Neto when off duty on the weekends. He was about my age and were "primo hermanos", first cousins, but we considered each other brothers.

After several months at Fort Bliss, I was given orders to

report to duty in the G2 section of the Korean Military Advisory Group (KMAG) in Seoul, Korea. I was overjoyed at getting those orders because I wanted to travel to another foreign country besides Mexico. I flew from El Paso to San Francisco, California, where I was able to stay for several days awaiting my military flight to Seoul Korea. I enjoyed my brief visit to the beautiful city of San Francisco and made plans to revisit the city in the future, never dreaming that one day I would wind up living and teaching in the San Francisco East Bay Area, across from that lovely city.

I arrived in Seoul, South Korea, in October of 1960. It was exciting being there. The U.S. Army base was in the center of the city. There was much to do. I enjoyed hanging out with my KMAG buddies at bars and restaurants around town. The Korean people were friendly, and I enjoyed learning about their culture and eating their food! One of the benefits of being part of the KMAG was access to a jeep on weekends to use to travel to visit museums and historical sites around town or out of town. I was also able to visit one of my high school buddies, Johnny Sepulveda, who was stationed a few hours' drive from Seoul at the US Army base in Yongsun.

I was given security clearance and therefore my responsibilities in the G2 section of the KMAG included logging in all secret intelligence reports coming in from the CIA and other intelligence sources about political developments within Korea and in Vietnam and other parts of Asia. After logging in those reports, I would hand carry them to the Commanding General's office. The job offered me a fascinating learning experience about the secret US political and military politics taking place in those countries, especially in Vietnam.

I learned that a student revolution had taken place several months before my arrival in South Korea. It took place during April of 1960 against the government of President Syngman Rhee. Elections were subsequently held and won by the Korean Democratic Party. But the military was not pleased because the new civilian government took away the power it had been able to exercise during the Rhee government.

In the early morning hours of May 16, 1961, we received orders to mobilize and prepare for possible combat. The reason was that the South Korean Army had undertaken a coup d'état led by General Park Chung-hee that overthrew the democratic government of South Korea. The rationale for the coup was that the civilian government was soft on communism and that their country needed a strong anti-communist government to prevent North Korea from breaking the 1953 Armistice that temporarily stopped the Korean War conflict and invading South Korea again. But the coup was a manifestation of the military's desire to once again exercise power in the South Korean government.

The coup raised critical questions in my mind about the role of our military and our government. I wondered why we were not ordered to stop the coup to prevent a military dictatorship from taking place. After all, we were there to defend the democratic government of one of our Asian allies. I later learned that President Kennedy's administration ordered the U.S. Commanding General not to stop the coup. The U.S.

government went on to support the South Korean military dictatorship of General Park until his assassination 30 years later.

I learned that during the time of the coup in May of 1961, President Kennedy had authorized sending 400 Special Forces troops, under the guise of "military advisors", to engage in covert warfare against the North Vietnam Revolutionary Army under the leadership of Ho Chi Minh. It marked the beginning of the Vietnam War. But it remained a "secret war" until about three years later.

About 4 months later, on September 16, 1961, after undergoing the coup d'état experience, I was able to take an R & R trip (Rest and Recuperation) to Tokyo, Japan. It was basically a paid weeks' vacation that U.S. soldiers were given for being stationed in a combat zone. The Korean War had never officially ended because a Treaty was never agreed upon between the North and the South. There was only a cease-fire agreement by way of an Armistice in 1953, so war conditions still existed.

Getting to Tokyo, however, was no fun because the small army propeller plane I was in flew into a horrendous typhoon (as hurricanes are called that take place in the Pacific Ocean) on the way to Tokyo. I remember the pilot telling us to hang in there tough and that the only way to survive was for him to fly into the "eye" of the typhoon. I thought perhaps my time on earth had come to an end. It was a scary experience but thank God the pilot did it and we made it out of that typhoon. After making a hard landing at the Tokyo military airport, the pilot yelled out for us to make a fast exit and run like hell for cover in the nearby huge airplane hangar. Wind and rain came down on us, but luckily the typhoon did not actually hit Tokyo but changed direction toward the city of Osaka, about 250 miles away, where it did terrible damage. I found out later that many lives were lost and hundreds of homes destroyed. The typhoon was named "Nancy" and was listed as one of the worst to ever hit Japan. Tokyo was spared any major damage and I was thankful to be alive after the scary typhoon experience. Needless to say, I enjoyed my R & R to the fullest with lots of good sake and sushi! Like the Korean people, I also found the Japanese to be friendly and respectful people. I was pleasantly surprised, given that I was a U.S. soldier, and I was welcomed and treated so well after the U.S. had dropped two atomic bombs on Japan during WWII.

During the time in Tokyo, I was able to reflect on my experience and to seriously ponder my future plans. After the coup d'état, I lost much of my earlier enthusiasm to pursue a military career. I questioned the US government's support of the military dictatorship and its decision to start the War in Vietnam. When I returned to duty in Seoul, South Korea, I was told to volunteer to go to Vietnam and become part of the Vietnam Military Advisory Group. But I refused.

I was only 20 years old at the time and a college drop out. I had not yet developed a critical political consciousness to enable me to articulate a critique of U.S. Foreign Policy or the coup d'état in South Korea, or the start of the Vietnam War. But it did start me thinking more critically about those issues and I did not agree with what was taking place in Vietnam.

I decided to think about other options instead of a military career. I gave college another try after completion of my tour of duty. I signed up for a University of Maryland Correspondence course and I started going to the army base library to start serious readings to prove to myself that I had the intellectual capacity for college. I picked out the classic book "Crime and Punishment" by the famous Russian writer Fyodor Dostoevsky. It was a very challenging read. I read it three times and finally on the 4th time reading it, I understood it! I also enjoyed reading Shakespeare. I thought to myself that something was rotten, not in Denmark, as Shakespeare had written in Hamlet, one of his famous plays, but that it was rotten elsewhere, in Vietnam and in Washington D.C. After getting through all that difficult reading, I felt I was a damn smart Mexican!

I shared my critical political questions about the coup d'état with several fellow soldiers in our barracks. The word got around. I started being harassed by one of the sergeants of our KMAG unit. During inspections he would go out of his way to criticize me, for example, not having my bunk area clean enough or that my bunk bed had no wrinkles in it. Finally, I could not take it anymore and I challenged him. The result was that I was punished with an "Article 15" for behavior inappropriately expressed against a superior officer. I was put on two weeks of restriction to my barracks. That was the straw that broke the camel's back. I firmly decided against a military career and made definite plans to return to college.

Unfortunately, my college plans were put on hold. When I was near to completion of my 2-year tour of duty, President Kennedy extended the duty of all military personnel due to the "Berlin Crisis". The Soviet Union had demanded the immediate withdrawal of U.S. forces from West Berlin. Military conflict against the Russians became a possibility. Instead of getting my discharge papers, I received orders to report to duty at Fort Belvoir, Virginia. But not to the Army Intelligence G2 section. No doubt my critical questioning of the coup d'état and the covert Vietnam War had something to do with it. I was given the job of a regular clerk typist in the headquarters of a U.S. Army Engineering Battalion.

There was a positive to my new assignment. Fort Belvoir was a stone's throw to Washington, D.C. It became my first opportunity to visit the nation's capital with all its museums and historic sites. I especially enjoyed the famous Abraham Lincoln Memorial from where Dr. Martin Luther King, Jr. would later give his "I have a Dream" speech during the historic March on Washington. He gave his speech approximately a year after getting my Honorable discharge from the U.S. Army in the Spring of 1962.

Around the time of the March on Washington, the Vietnam War had evolved from President Kennedy's covert war to his successor President Lyndon Johnson's overt war. The U.S. Congress, in addition to giving Johnson the authorization to continue the war, also passed a Vietnam War Era Veteran G.I. bill to provide funds for high education for all those who served in other combat areas in the military during the war. It was not limited to those who served in Vietnam. I was pleased I was eligible, and it gave me further motivation to return to college.

Chapter 4

Becoming a Student Activist: East LA Walkouts

Author in center photograph taken during East Los Angeles High School Blowout Protest, March 3, 1968. (Raul Ruiz photo)

I was 22 years old at the time I received my honorable discharge from the U.S. Army. I returned to Los Angeles and moved in with my parents temporarily until I could find a job and a place of my own to stay. My plans to return to college had to be put on hold because it was the middle of the spring semester, so I applied for admission in the Fall semester of 1962 at Los Angeles City College.

My job search did not go well so my stay with my parents was longer than I had wanted. My stepmother was no longer a problem for me, but it continued to be difficult to deal with my father's alcoholism. It depressed me and after having a shouting confrontation with him about his drinking I called a hotline for families of alcoholics to find out what I could do to get him to stop drinking. I was told that I had to understand alcoholism was an illness. It had never entered my mind that it was. That knowledge enabled me to treat my father with kindness as opposed to anger. I tried to convince him to return to Alcoholic Anonymous (AA) to help him deal with his illness. But I did not succeed.

I finally got a job, thanks to George Hirai, one of my close high school friends who worked as a "delivery boy" for an international architectural and engineering firm named Daniel, Mann, Johnson, and Mendenhall (DMJM) that was located on Wilshire Blvd, the "wall street" sector of Los Angeles. He said there was an opening for another delivery "boy". So I applied. I got the job because the personnel guy who interviewed me was a former FBI agent who was impressed with my Army Intelligence background. It was a full-time job that paid well enough for me to afford a small apartment. I found one that was walking distance to the job on Wilshire Blvd. and to the Los Angeles City College campus. It had a very small kitchen and a room that was a combination bedroom and living room, the bed folded into the wall after use.

I started a challenging schedule of taking a full load of classes in the evenings after working 8 hours a day. There was little time for a social life or political activism. I was able to maintain a B average.

At my job, I made rapid progress in working my way up the ladder of the firm. I went from "delivery boy" to mailroom clerk. And from there I was promoted to an administrative assistant job in the firm's legal international department. My job was to closely work with the company lawyers to keep track of their contracts for the U.S. Agency for International Development. I had been thinking about going to law school, but the experience working with the lawyers was not exciting, actually boring. I put my thinking about law school on hold.

At this time, my father continued his heavy drinking and one day when I was visiting him he cried out in the bathroom. I ran in to help him and discovered he was vomiting blood. He collapsed and I put him in his car and drove him to the emergency room at the LA County General Hospital. All the folks in the waiting room were poor Mexican Americans and African Americans. After a long wait, a doctor finally arrived to check him out. He told me to take him back home because it was not serious. He was wrong. On the way down in the elevator, he resumed vomiting blood and passed out. Nurses helped me pick him up and check him in at the ER admissions desk. As he was being wheeled down the hallway, he waved his arms erratically, kicked his legs up in the air. I got the impression he was trying to fight his way out of the bad situation. I went to him and he told me "I gotta go work and pay my bills". Those would be his last words. I left him in the hospital for overnight observation and tests.

The next morning, I had a final exam in biology and called the hospital after the exam to check up on him. A doctor picked up the phone and said three words, "your father expired". Expired? Damn, he could not say "sorry to tell you but your father has passed away"? Or something like that? I guess my father was simply another poor Mexican to him, no big deal.

I immediately drove to the hospital remembering his last words to me. When I arrived, another doctor explained that his death was caused by the rupturing of his stomach lining due to his alcoholism. When he did not have money to buy liquor, he would drink "after shave" stuff that had alcohol content. No doubt doing significant damage to his stomach lining. The heavy drinking had taken its toll. He was only 49 years old.

His death was a major blow to me and without a family support system of siblings and other family, I felt extremely lonely. He and I were never that close due to his alcoholism. But I needed someone to fill the void in my life. I got married soon after his death. The marriage proved to be a mistake and did not last long, although it produced my first two wonderful children, Carlos and Marina.

I graduated with an Associate of Arts Degree in June of 1964 from LA City College. At work, I was offered the job of running the office of the DMJM Corporation in Hawaii with a salary of $60,000 a year. Needless to say, having been a barrio boy who had lived in poverty, I was overjoyed. I could not even comprehend how much money that really was and never dreamed I could earn more than much, especially at the age of 25! Plus, I now had a family to support. Without much thought I quickly accepted the offer.

However, after a couple of days, I reflected on my decision to accept it. I could not sleep. The job in Hawaii would be a radical departure from the plans I had made to complete my college education and then serve the Mexican American community as one of their leaders. I concluded I had to keep true to my plans and continue to work my way through college.

I met with one of the partners of the firm who made me the offer and told him I was grateful for the opportunity, but that I had decided to continue with my college education and future plans. His response was not very positive. In his mind I had ceased to be a company man. I got the message that I would not get any more promotions. So I resigned and found another job near the California State University at Los Angeles (CSULA) campus where I decided to transfer to pursue the BA degree in political science. The new job title was "Expeditor" in the purchasing department of another engineering corporation by the name of C.F. Braun.

I started attending CSULA on a part time basis in the fall of 1964 because I had to work full time. It was not possible to carry a full academic load in the evening as I had done at LA City College because course work was much more demanding. When the U.S. Congress passed the Vietnam War Era Veterans G.I. Bill in 1966, I was able to quit my full time job and work part time on campus because the G.I. Bill covered my tuition and books. Most importantly, working part time gave me the time to become a student activist.

By this time in my life, I was becoming more critically aware of the problems facing my people and the reality of living in a racist society. I became involved in the anti-Vietnam war movement after learning that Mexican Americans were dying on the battlefield at a proportionately higher rate than other soldiers. In 1965, I participated in one of the first major mass protests against the war in Vietnam. It was my first act as a student activist. President Lyndon Johnson was in town and staying at the Hyatt Regency Century Plaza Hotel near UCLA. I was among the thousands who welcomed him to the city with cries of "end the war now!" and picket signs with slogans like "make love, not war", "when the rich make war, it's the poor who die!", "peace is patriotic", "stop the war, bring the troops home!", "give peace a chance!". The majority of protestors were white, young, and mostly college students. This was due to the fact that the anti-war movement at that time was largely a white student movement. But some folks of color were also part of the protest.

It was a loud but peaceful nonviolent protest. But the army of LA policemen assigned to guard the President were not impressed. The policemen charged into the waves of protestors swinging their clubs and smashing heads, I went to the aid of an elderly white lady in a wheelchair who had been knocked down and I picked her up. I was angry at the cop for attacking her and having no respect for the elderly. In disbelief of what I was witnessing, I questioned what happened to the 1st Amendment of the U.S. Constitution? This protest action contributed to my increasing radicalization.

Between 1965 and 1968 I became a participant in campus student protest actions against the war that was organized by the Students for a Democratic Society (SDS). Around the same time, I also became a member of the United Mexican American Students (UMAS), a new organization on campus that emerged in late 1967. I became friends with Lillian Roybal, another member of UMAS who was one of the daughters of Congressman Edward Roybal. At that time, he was one of only two Mexican American members of the U.S. Congress. The other was Henry González, the first one to be elected in Texas.

She invited me to dinner at her family's home where I met the Congressman. We talked politics and I was impressed with his liberal progressive views, and he was pleased that I shared them. He encouraged me to become involved in community organizations where I could get to know their leadership and thus open the path toward eventually running for political office. I decided I would do that and planned to pursue a career in politics as a U.S. Congressman.

My college education up to this point had taken place without any course work that included knowledge about the Mexican American experience. We were an invisible people throughout the society at that time in spite of the fact that Mexican Americans had served with bravery in World War II and Korea, were doing it again in Vietnam, and had made the difference in the 1960 election of John F. Kennedy to the presidency of the United States.

A story on the front page of the Los Angeles Times about

the Ford Foundation donating a huge research grant to UCLA for research on the Asian American Experience caught my eye. I wrote a letter to the editor of the newspaper stating that I was happy to learn of the grant and praised the Asian American community leaders and scholars responsible for getting the grant. I criticized Mexican American leaders and scholars for not doing the same.

One of those leaders harshly responded to my letter with his letter to the editor. He was a lawyer named Carlos Borja who was on the staff of the State of California Attorney General. Basically, he said I did not know what I was talking about and should not assume that the Mexican American leadership was not concerned about the issue. He wrote me a personal letter afterwards saying that perhaps his letter to the editor was a bit too harsh and invited me to have lunch with him. We had a pleasant talk and he invited me to attend meetings of his community organization. Most importantly, he encouraged me to think about law school and recommended that I transfer to Occidental College, a more prestigious college than Cal State LA, and because there was a sociologist on the faculty who was doing research on the Mexican American experience. His name was Paul Sheldon. Borja thought I could get a full scholarship because private colleges had more money than state colleges.

I made an appointment with Professor Sheldon, and he was gracious and supportive. He walked me over to the college Admission office where I was given a vocabulary test. After the test the administrator told me that I could not be admitted because the test results indicated I did not have the vocabulary required for admission. In retrospect, I should have scheduled the test for a later date so I could have prepared for it. To put it mildly I was very disappointed. I had been dreaming about attending Occidental on a full scholarship since Borja had recommended it.

Many years later, after joining the faculty at UC Berkeley, I was invited to give a keynote speech at a Occidental College commemoration of Dr. Ernesto Galarza, one of my mentors, who had attended the college as an undergraduate in the 1920s. I seriously thought about mentioning that incident about me not having the vocabulary needed for admission into Occidental. But I didn't do it because Dr. Galarza's widow and two daughters were in the audience. I took the high ground because it would have taken away from the honoring of Dr. Galarza.

I graduated with a B.A. in political science from Cal State LA in the winter semester of 1967 and stayed there to study for the M.A. degree. The Civil Rights and Anti-War Movements were going strong and socialist revolutions were taking place in the Third World. I closely followed the news of those movements and revolutions, and they contributed to increasing my radicalization. I continued to be part of the anti-war movement. I also became a supporter of the civil rights movement led by Dr. King and made contact with members of that movement's Student Non-Violent Coordinating Committee (SNCC). I also made contact with the farm worker movement led by César Chávez and Dolores Huerta.

In the Spring semester of 1968, I was elected president of the UMAS student organization. I did not plan on running for that office because I thought an undergraduate should be president. In particular, Maria Baeza was one of the undergrads who impressed me. I thought she was a strong leader and extremely bright. But she told me I should be the president because "the guys" would not listen to her. Plus, she was not a citizen and feared the loss of her green card and deportation back to Mexico if she was arrested at a future protest action. So, she convinced me to run and I told her I would if she promised to run for vice-president. She agreed. One of my first acts as UMAS president was to form a collective leadership committee that would have a gender balance. It included Maria as vice-president and two other women and two males.

Next, I formed a Black-Brown coalition with the Black Student Union on campus. In the process I connected with the Student Nonviolent Coordinating Committee of the civil rights movement. Our coalition requested that the campus administration provide us with a joint space for each organization's office and where meetings could take place. We were "given" a small house next to the campus and we named it the "Black-Brown House". At one of our first joint meetings, we agreed to invite the heavyweight champion of the world, Muhammed Ali, to speak on campus against the war in Vietnam. He had been drafted but refused to serve during the Vietnam War for religious reasons. His championship title was taken away by the World Boxing Association for his refusal. It was decided that the BSU president and I would be Ali's honorary bodyguards as a symbolic show of solidarity between UMAS and BSU. I was proud to accompany Ali across campus to the football stadium where he spoke. He towered over me and I looked up at him and said "hey champ, you should be my bodyguard!" He looked down at me, put his arm around me, clenched his fist, and smiled.

In the days following Ali's dramatic anti-war speech, we jointly decided to propose the establishment of Departments of African American Studies and Mexican American Studies. I had a part time job working as a graduate student assistant for Professor Ralph Guzman, the only Mexican American faculty in the political science department and one of a handful in the entire campus. I discussed our UMAS plans with him for a Mexican American Studies department. His response was positive, and he offered to be of help. I set up an UMAS committee headed by Maria Baeza to work with Professor Guzman on writing up a proposal to the administration.

Other UMAS priorities during my presidency included engagement and support of local community struggles. We got funding from the college administration to set up a community center in East Los Angeles where UMAS members could provide tutoring for high school students and help prepare them for college. Our center was connected to the college equal opportunity program (EOP). We also organized food and clothing drives for the United Farmworker Union during their long strike against the grape growers. On campus we held community conferences, cultural, and political events. Oscar Martinez was the UMAS member who played a key role in organizing the community conferences.

Participants at those events included Luis Valdez and his Teatro Campesino. Dr. Ernesto Galarza was a noted educator and labor activist. Before César Chávez emerged, he had been a leading organizer of the Southern Tenant Farmer

Union in Arkansas. That union was comprised of a largely African American membership that was led by Socialist H. L. Mitchell. Later he organized Mexican American farm workers in California as one of the leaders of the Farm Labor Union. César's father was a member of Dr. Galarza's Union.

Reies Lopez Tijerina, leader of the Land Grants Movement in New Mexico and Rodolfo ``Corky'' Gonzalez, leader of the Crusade for Justice in Colorado also spoke at our campus UMAS conferences.

Dr. Octavio Romano V, co-founder and editor of the Quinto Sol Journal at UC Berkeley was also one of our guest speakers. It was the first intellectual journal that featured both scholars and community activists and writers. Dr. Juan Martinez, who was a key faculty supporter of the 1968 Third World Student Strike at San Francisco State College also spoke. I spoke to both of them, as well as Dr. Galarza about becoming faculty in our new Mexican American Studies Department. None of them expressed interest.

All these events and speakers greatly contributed to my knowledge about the issues being confronted by Mexican Americans and specifically connected me with organizations and individuals with whom I would later work with in the organizing of the Chicano Civil Rights Movement and La Raza Unida Party.

Another speaker we invited to campus was a high school teacher by the name of Sal Castro. He spoke about the racism and unequal education his students faced at Lincoln High School and at other segregated East Los Angeles barrio high schools. He asked us for support in organizing student protest actions, like student walkouts, that would force the Los Angeles Board of Education to make reforms in the schools that would result in equal education. In particular, that would eliminate racist practices and attitudes on the part of white teachers. Also result in a curriculum that would have courses on Mexican American history and culture. Castro inspired us to take action and we voted unanimously to become part of the struggle for educational change that Castro called for. It became the key local community issue for UMAS on our campus and at other colleges and universities in the Los Angeles area, and eventually throughout the Southwest. I was also motivated to play a role in organizing the "Walk Outs" because I well-remembered my experience being a victim of the racist tracking system at Belmont High School, one of the target barrio schools. It was a system that historically excluded Mexican and African American students from the academic major offering courses required for admission to 4-year colleges and universities. Black and Brown males were automatically given the "Industrial Arts" major that offered courses in wood shop and auto shop instead of the Academic major that offered courses like algebra, geometry, and chemistry, etc. Female students were given Home Economics or Business majors. Only white and Asian students were given the Academic majors required for college admissions.

In addition to demanding the end of that racist system, we came up with over a hundred other demands for educational reforms in the ELA (East Lost Angeles) high schools including the creation of courses in Mexican American history and culture. The demands were presented to the Los Angeles Board of Education. The majority of the members of the Board were not supportive. We then made the decision to call for student walkouts from the barrio high schools to dramatize the demands we made to the Board of Education.

It took us several months to organize the student walkouts. Many of the meetings took place at the Epiphany Episcopal Church in the Lincoln Heights barrio where I lived at that time. The pastor was a good white liberal by the name of Father John Luce who was the "black sheep" of one of the leading 'blue blood" east coast wealthy families who were industrialists and owners of Time-Life magazine and other Capitalist endeavors. Although I can't document it, Father Luce probably also made significant financial contributions toward our organizing efforts and made possible contributions by others who supported our cause. He also gave space to several of my co-organizers for them to produce an "underground" community newspaper they named "La Raza". The editor was Elizer Risco, a Cuban immigrant active in the progressive religious network involved with issues in communities of color. One of the reporters was student activist Raul Ruiz at Cal State LA who would become one of the leaders of La Raza Unida political party in Los Angeles. Ruiz also produced a smaller newspaper called "Chicano Student News" that focused on issues the walkouts would later address. Ruiz also became one of the prominent candidates of La Raza Unida Party who challenged the heavily favored Democrat, Richard Alattore, in Los Angeles. Both La Raza and the Chicano Student News newspapers did an excellent job of reporting on the bad conditions of the schools, the high dropout rates, and the problems faced by students who had racist teachers, etc. The report was successful in educating parents and community activists about those issues that were never reported in the LA Times and other mainstream media.

On the morning of March 3rd, 1968, students started to walk out of the schools. According to the LA Times over 10,000 students walked out of four barrio high schools during a week and half resulting in the disruption of business as usual in the Los Angeles city school district. Unknown to us at that time, it was the largest mass protest by Mexican Americans in the history of the United States. We also did not know that those of us involved in the organizing of the walkouts were under heavy surveillance by undercover LAPD and county Sheriff Deputies from their respective intelligence divisions. Nor did we know that they were part of the FBI Counterintelligence Program (COINTELPRO) network that included all police departments throughout the nation, especially in those cities with visible anti-war and civil rights movements. I did not discover these facts until years later when I obtained documents from the FBI through the Freedom of Information Act. Those documents contained information submitted by the undercover police who had conducted the surveillance of those of us who organized the 1968 ELA student walkouts.

Approximately two months after the walkouts, the Los Angeles County Grand Jury indicted me and twelve other male civil rights activists for "conspiracy to disrupt the city's public schools". Los Angeles police and LA County sheriffs were ordered to arrest us.

I was arrested in the early morning hours when I was writing a paper for a graduate seminar on "International Communism" being taught by an anti-communist professor.

The police, wearing bullet proof vests, broke into my apartment and with guns drawn ordered me to fall on the floor so they could handcuff me. They asked me where my weapons were located. They ran upstairs looking for weapons and terrorized my family where they had been sleeping. Another officer saw a stack of books on my kitchen table where I was typing my paper. The books were authored by Karl Marx, Vladimir Lenin, and Leon Trotsky. He yelled, "we got the goods on this damn communist agitator!" I was learning about communism, but at that time I was far from being one. The comment, however, reflected the anti-communist mentality of J. Edgar Hoover, the Director of the FBI, and the majority of "law and order" political leaders from the US President on down.

I was taken outside of my house and one of the officers told me that he would take the handcuffs off if I wanted to make a run for it. I had a hunch I would be shot. I declined the offer. I was taken to the County Jail and thrown into a cell with men who had been arrested for felony crimes ranging from murder and armed robbery to rape and forging checks. None of them could believe that I was their cellmate for only organizing nonviolent student protests! I told them I could not believe it either. In fact, I was still in shock that I had been arrested.

We each faced 66 years in prison for the felony "crime" of conspiring to organize nonviolent protest. Our attorneys decided to take our case to the California Supreme Court. But on the way there, 2 years later, the California State Appellate Court ruled in 1970 that we were innocent by virtue of the First Amendment to the U.S. Constitution. I thank God for that amendment and the civil liberties we enjoy every day. If it were not for that amendment, which as you know, grants us freedom of speech, I would be in prison today.

The others arrested were Sal Castro, teacher at Lincoln High School; Elizer Risco, the editor of the underground La Raza Newspaper; David Sanchez, the Prime Minister of the Brown Berets, and Ralph Ramirez, Carlos Montes, and Fred Lopez, also members of the Brown Berets. Sanchez, Ramirez, and Lopez had been students in the first Chicano Studies class I taught when I was a graduate student at Cal State L.A. The rest of the 13 were Patricio Sanchez, Joe Razo, Richard Vigil, Gilberto Cruz Olmeda, and Henry Gomez, all community civil rights activists; and Moctezuma Esparza, a leader of UMAS at UCLA. None of the 13 arrested were high school students or women.

In actuality, there were more than the 13 "conspirators". And there were many women who participated in the organizing of the student Walkouts. Some of them were much more involved in the organizing than I was. I always wondered why they were not indicted. I assumed I was indicted because I was the president of UMAS and my arrest may have seemed logical to the power structure if the intent was to intimidate the rank and file of the organization. I could understand why Sal Castro was arrested given that he was the key source of inspiration to the high school students and those of us who organized the walkouts.

With the exception of two Brown Berets who were at the Poor People's march in Washington, D.C., and another who disappeared, ten of us were arrested and imprisoned on May 31st, 1968. Of those arrested, 8 were put in a group cell at the recently built "glass house" downtown city jail. They decided to participate as a group in a hunger strike to demonstrate the injustice of our indictments and arrests. Sal Castro and I were put into the LA County Jail, but in separate cells with men who had been arrested for felony crimes. My cellmates had been arrested for armed robbery, passing bad checks, and selling drugs. I decided not to go on a hunger strike because I needed to maintain my strength in the event I had to deal with some physical confrontation with one or more of my cellmates.

They asked me what I did, and they could not believe I was there for organizing nonviolent student protests. They thought I might be an undercover cop planted in their cell to get information about them. But I finally put them at ease after telling them that if I were an undercover cop, I would have given them the story that I had also engaged in one of the felony crimes they were arrested for and not for simply organizing nonviolent student protest. They asked me to explain why I was there in the cell with them if that was all I did. I replied that it would take a book for me to adequately explain it. Years later, my book *Youth, Identity, Power: The Chicano Movement* became that book. This book is a more personal account of my live experience that led to my 1968 imprisonment on charges of conspiracy in both the making of the high school student walkouts and my involvement in the making of the Chicano Civil Rights Movement, La Raza Unida Party, and the making of the New Left throughout the U.S.

Afterward, the cellmate arrested on drug charges, a tough looking Chicano, offered me a job selling drugs. He said "when you get out, contact me and I'll give you a job that comes with good benefits, shiny new car and all the sexy women you want".

We were only imprisoned for about a week before Senator Eugene McCarthy, then running for U.S. President against Robert Kennedy for the Democratic nomination, donated the bail money for our release. But to me it seemed like a lifetime imprisonment. When my attorney told me that if convicted of the conspiracy charges, we could get up to 66 years in prison, I worried about what would happen to my two young children, Carlitos and Marina, ages 3 and 1 at the time.

After our release on bail, we were invited to celebrate at a dinner at a Mexican restaurant on North Broadway in Lincoln Heights. Rene Nuñez, the director of the "ELA Clearing House", a center that dealt with college admissions for Chicano/a youth, gave me an abrazo and told me "Carlos, you are now a hero!", but I did not feel like a hero. I felt like an angry victim of injustice who had a possible 66-year term in prison hanging over his head.

Oscar Acosta approached me and gave me his business card that said he was a "Chicano lawyer" and offered to defend me in court. But I was not impressed with him after he told me that our emerging movement for educational reform needed heroes and that I and the other 12 who were indicted should plead guilty. My response to him was that I preferred to be free to continue to organize the struggle for justice and educational reforms and not serve a lifetime behind iron bars. I turned him down on his offer to defend me. I instead chose a Jewish lawyer from the ACLU by the name of Paul Posner. He was highly recommended by Professor Ralph Guzman. Four of my "co-conspirators" Brown Berets also decided not to have Acosta as their lawyer and they also chose Paul Posner as their lawyer to represent them in court. Sal Castro, perceived as the key co-conspirator by the police, chose a Mexican American lawyer by the name of Herman Sillas as his attorney.

Tensions within the 13 "co-conspirators" emerged between those who chose Acosta versus those of us who chose other lawyers. I was warned not to "make trouble for Acosta" by one of those being defended by him. Luckily, the various lawyers representing us were able to convince Acosta to work together to build a sound legal defense. They decided on a strategy that would postpone a trial and instead pursue a path leading to the State Supreme court as a freedom of speech case based on the 1st Amendment to the U.S. Constitution. Our case became officially known as the "Castro, et. al. vs. the People". In the community it became known as the case of the "East LA 13". On the way to the State Supreme Court, our lawyers argued it before the State Appellate Court. We were out on bail for 2 years until the Appellate Court ruled we were innocent of the conspiracy charges by virtue of the 1st Amendment to the U.S. Constitution that warranted Freedom of Speech.

After release from prison on bail, I returned to my graduate studies and during two years on bail, I served out my term as President of UMAS, and served as the acting chair of the new department of Mexican American Studies with the title of "Acting Coordinator". I also was admitted to the political science PhD program at Stanford University and to the department of Government at the Claremont Graduate School (later to be renamed the Claremont Graduate University). When I visited the Stanford campus to meet the faculty, I got the feeling that I would only be a token Affirmative Action admit, so I decided to attend Claremont where I got the feeling I would be taken more seriously. I received a part time faculty appointment at Pitzer College, one of the undergraduate Claremont colleges.

In the Spring of 1969, I became involved in the organizing of a California statewide conference on Mexican American Studies and equal opportunity for access to higher education for Mexican Americans that had been planned by Rene Nuñez. We did not know at that time the conference would become a historical one. Prior to the conference there had not been any effort to deal with the significant issues on those subjects. The conference took place at the campus of the University of California at Santa Barbara. I served as a member of the conference steering committee. We produced a book length document entitled "The Plan de Santa Barbara". It was both a radical manifesto and a blueprint for the creation of Mexican American Studies programs, departments, and centers at all the institutions of higher education in California.

The participants of the conference were the handful of Mexican American faculty and staff at those institutions and student leaders of organizations on campuses of the University of California, the State College system and Community Colleges. And most importantly, it included the key leadership of the emerging Chicano student movement. Although not on the agenda of the conference, student leaders decided to rename all the student organizations they represented as chapters of the "Movimiento Estudiantil Chicano de Aztlan" or MEChA. In California, the previous organizational names had been UMAS (UNITED MEXICAN AMERICAN STUDENTS) and MASC (MEXICAN AMERICAN STUDENT CONFEDERATION), and

MASA (MEXICAN AMERICAN STUDENT ASSOCIATION. The thrust for the name MEChA came from the student activists, led by Ysidro Macias, a leader of MASC at UC Berkeley, who had attended an earlier national conference held prior to the Santa Barbara Conference. It was held in Denver, Colorado, and had been hosted by the Crusade for Justice. The conference was called "The National Chicano Liberation Conference" and it produced a manifesto entitled "El Plan de Aztlan".

The Chicano identity became a focal point of the conference as it had been in the Denver conference. Prior to those conferences the prevailing identity had been "Mexican American" without a hyphen. The first time I heard "Chicano" or saw it on picket signs was during the 1968 East Los Angeles high school student walkouts. I cherish a photo of me next to a high school student who had a sign saying, "Chicano Power".

After the Santa Barbara Conference, I stepped down from the acting department chair responsibilities at Cal State LA and began my graduate work for the PhD at the Claremont Graduate School. To make ends meet, I obtained a part time job teaching at Pitzer College, one of the undergraduate Claremont colleges.

Chapter 5

The Struggle for Chicano/a & Ethnic Studies in the Academy

Marching with UC Berkeley faculty and students, calling for divestment of UC system investments in apartheid government of South Africa. (1980s)

When I served as President of the United Mexican American Students (UMAS) in 1968, I asked Professor Ralph Guzman to support our efforts to create a department of Mexican American Studies at CSULA. He agreed to write up a proposal for its creation and when approved, to serve as its first department chair. After I finished my term as UMAS president, it turned out that he wrote a proposal for a Mexican American Studies Center instead. He did it without discussing it with the students or me. The main distinction between a Center and a Department is that a department is funded to hire its own faculty and has the power to develop its own curriculum whereas a Center does not. A Center draws its faculty from existing traditional departments who teach courses from their own department curriculum. Most importantly, Guzman's proposal was based only on traditional academic criteria whereas the students and I wanted a department that included an explicit community activist component. I think he meant well perhaps because he felt that a Center was more feasible since it would not require the allocation of additional funding and thus easier to receive the approval of the Academic Senate and the college administration.

During the summer of 1968, Monte Perez, the new UMAS president who succeeded me, requested that I facilitate a meeting between the new UMAS leadership and Guzman to convince him to rewrite the proposal for a department as UMAS had originally requested. I decided to do it, although it was awkward for me. As the past president of UMAS, I felt loyalty to the students. But I also felt loyalty to Guzman because I considered him a mentor and he had arranged for an ACLU lawyer to defend me against the charges of conspiracy that I faced after the 1968 high school student walkouts. Unfortunately, the meeting was extremely tense and Guzman refused to rewrite the proposal. He told the students he could not continue to work with them. After the meeting, the new UMAS leadership asked me to take over the task of pushing for the department as originally requested.

I met with Dr. Ken Martyn, the Vice President for Academic Affairs to inform him that UMAS requested that I replace Professor Guzman due to their disagreement over the structure of Mexican American Studies. Luckily, he had already approved the request from the Black Student Union for the establishment of a department of Black Studies, so he did not see a problem with the creation of a department of Mexican American Studies instead of a Center as proposed by Guzman. He approved the creation of both departments and directed the Dean of the School of Letters and Science, Dr. Leonard Mathy, to appoint me as the acting chair with the title of "Coordinator" since graduate students could not serve as official department chairs.

Although Dr. Martin had officially approved the department during the summer, the formal announcement of the creation of both the Mexican American and the African American Studies departments was made by the Los Angeles Times on January 9, 1969, in an article with the title "Cal State LA, Launches First Departments for Minorities" with photos of me and the Coordinator of the African American Studies Department. Dean Mathy was quoted as saying that the departments were hurriedly approved to avoid the "danger of student unrest" but also because they agreed it was important to have a curriculum on "an aspect of society that had been ignored in higher education".

In contrast to the experience at San Francisco State College where Mexican American students and other students of color did not get approval for departments. They declared a "Third World" student strike and engaged in violent confrontations with the police in late 1968. This strike was followed by a similar student strike at the University of California, Berkeley, in 1969. Students demanded the creation of a Third World College. Our experience was characterized by peaceful negotiations. The administration had respect for me due to the good word given by two Mexican American staff members. One of them was Maria Lopez who had served as the secretary to CSULA President Greenlee, and afterward as secretary to the Vice President for Academic Affairs Dr. Martyn. The other was Felix Gutierrez, Jr. who was the Assistant Director of the campus EPIC Program and served as our UMAS Advisor along with Professor Ralph Guzman.

My first task as acting chair was to immediately develop the first two courses for the department. I decided that the department's first two courses should be on Mexican American history and Mexican American politics. I asked Gilbert Gonzales, a graduate student in history, to create and teach the history course. I created and taught the course on politics that I entitled "Contemporary Politics of the Southwest". A book on Mexican American or Latino politics had not yet been published. So, I used "North From Mexico" by Carey McWilliams, a white liberal lawyer who became the founder of the Nation magazine, as the main required text. Although his book was not centered on politics, it offered a historic context explaining the political powerlessness of Mexican Americans. I also compiled a xerox course reader of articles on some aspects of Mexican American politics. Gonzalez and I became the first two faculty (albeit part time since we were full time graduate students) of what turned out to be the first department of Mexican American Studies in the nation.

My next step was to make the effort to recruit Mexican Americans with Phds that could become permanent faculty for the department. And one that could become the permanent Chair of the department. Unfortunately, at that time in history, Mexican Americans with Phds were practically invisible in higher education. I contacted the handful whose published works I had read. Their names were George I. Sanchez (Education), Americo Paredes (Anthropology), Julian Samora (Sociology), and Ernesto Galarza (Economics). The first two were faculty at the University of Texas at Austin, Samora was at the University of Notre Dame, and Galarza was an independent scholar activist who did not hold any faculty appointment. None of them expressed an interest. I stayed in touch with all of them over the years, and eventually got to know them fairly well, especially the scholar activist Galarza whom I came to see as one of my mentors.

Professor Guzman recommended two other Mexican American scholars with Phds for me to contact. They were Octavio Romano at the University of California, Berkeley (Anthropology) and Juan Martinez at San Francisco State College (History). I discovered a third one at Smith College, an independent liberal arts women's college in Massachusetts. His name was Ramon Ruiz (History). I read his book on the Cuban Revolution that was required reading for a graduate seminar I took on that topic. I thought he was probably a Cuban American, but since he had a "Zapata mustache" (his photo was on the back cover) I thought maybe that he might be Mexican. So I called him. It turned out he was indeed a Mexican American who had obtained his PhD in history from UC Berkeley.

The interview visits by Romano and Martinez were meaningful to the students. Both were well aware of the 1968 East Los Angeles student walkouts and the Chicano Movement they ignited throughout the Southwest. But both decided against leaving their respective institutions and joining our faculty.

The visit by Ruiz unfortunately did not go well. He was a mainstream scholar and he felt very uncomfortable with the fact that he was being recruited by a graduate student, and not a bona fide faculty member or administrator. Maria Baeza and I took Ruiz to dinner and interviewed him. During the interview he understood why the students thought it important to have a department with a curriculum of courses on the Mexican American experience, but he made it clear that he would not allow students a voice in the decision-making process of the department. More unfortunately, he was not in agreement with the sentiments of UMAS that the department should have a community activist component. After our interview he joined the faculty in the department of history at UC San Diego where he became a prominent scholar of Mexican history.

EL PLAN DE SANTA BÁRBARA

During my tenure as acting chair of Mexican American Studies at CSULA, I became a founding member of the Chicano Coordinating Council on Higher Education (CCHE) and served as a member of its Steering Committee. CCHE was a small network of the few Mexican American faculty, staff, and student activists at colleges and universities across the state of California. It also included community activists who were involved in projects that encouraged Mexican American youth to think and plan for a college education. One of them was Rene Nuñez who played a key role in our steering committee. He was the Director of the East Los Angeles Clearing House, an outreach community program in East Los Angeles that helped Mexican American youth apply to college. At one of our meetings, he argued that we should host a statewide conference that would put pressure on those who controlled college and university affirmative action programs to include Mexican Americans, not just African Americans.

We organized a statewide conference that took place at the University of California, Santa Bárbara, in the Spring of 1969. The initial purpose of the conference was to put together a Mexican American master plan for higher education that would contribute to the inclusion of Mexican Americans and other Latinos in the Equal Opportunity Programs (EOP) at state college and the University of California campuses. At that time those programs were limited to African American youth. We later decided, however, that the master plan would also include the development of Mexican American Studies departments or programs.

We did not know at that time that the conference would be a historical one. Prior to the conference there had not been any large-scale effort to deal with those significant issues. The participants of the conference were the relative handful of Mexican American faculty and staff at those institutions. The majority were student activists, some of them who became the leadership of the emerging Chicano student movement. As previously introduced, these organizations included: UMAS chapters, the Mexican American Student Confederation (MASC), the Mexican

American Student Association (MASA), and the Mexican American Youth Organization (MAYO). Many of them had attended the Chicano Liberation Youth Conference in Denver, Colorado, hosted by the Crusade for Justice under the leadership of Rodolfo "Corky" Gonzalez. That conference took place a couple of months before our Santa Barbara conference. In keeping with the Chicano cultural nationalist "Plan de Aztlan" that was produced by the Denver conference, the students who had attended that conference called for all the student organizations they represented to rename their respective organizations the "Movimiento Estudiantil Chicano de Aztlan (MEChA).

In a special meeting held during the Santa Barbara conference by those students, led by Ysidro Macias, the leader of MASC at UC Berkeley, they engaged in deliberations about the name change with students and faculty and staff who did not attend the Denver conference. After a long discussion of the pros and cons of the name change, the majority of those in the meeting voted in favor of the name change. I was one of them. The students agreed they would propose the name change to their respective student organizations at their campus.

The handful of us who were faculty members at several campuses in California engaged in the process of developing Mexican American Studies programs and departments, decided we would rename them Chicano Studies. The nationalist Chicano identity and ideology became a focal point of the Santa Barbara conference as it had been in the Denver conference.

The proceedings of the conference were published by La Causa Publications, a local community press that was founded by civil rights activist Armando Valdez, and a member of our CCHE steering committee. It was a book length document entitled "El Plan de Santa Barbara: A Chicano Plan for Higher Education". It was both a radical manifesto and a blueprint for the organization of MEChA chapters and the creation of Chicano Studies programs, departments, and centers at all the institutions of higher education in California.

After the Santa Barbara Conference I was accepted into the PhD programs at Stanford University and the Claremont Graduate School for the fall semester of 1969. I had visited the Stanford campus for interviews with the political science faculty. The campus at that time was all white and I got the distinct impression that I was being accepted as a graduate student because they wanted me to be an affirmative action "window dressing". The faculty made it clear that they expected me to take on a dissertation topic of interest to one of them. I wrote a letter to the president of Stanford with copies to the political science faculty objecting to their paternalistic attitude and lack of interest in research of the Mexican American experience.

Despite the more conservative image of the Claremont Graduate School, I decided to accept their invitation to become a graduate student in political science. I believed I would get better support by their faculty to pursue my research agenda for my doctoral dissertation on the Mexican American experience. One of the reasons was because I knew a couple of the faculty fairly well. They had been visiting professors at CSULA.

I stepped down as acting department chair of the Cal State LA department and began my graduate work for the PhD in political science. I was awarded a fellowship that paid for my tuition, but to make ends meet, the Claremont faculty also arranged a part time teaching job for me at Pitzer College, one of the Claremont undergraduate colleges.

The Claremont Colleges were private and offered a whole different world than the public colleges that I had attended. The Claremont students were, with few exceptions, from the white upper middle and upper classes whereas those at the colleges I had attended were largely from the working class. The majority of the Mexican American students I taught At Cal State L.A. were low income and part of the Equal Opportunity Program (EOP). Those that I taught at Pitzer College were largely sons and daughters of professional parents, corporate CEO's, actors, and military officers. One of my students was the daughter of actor Burt Lancaster and another was the daughter of General Westmoreland who was the commanding general of U.S. forces during the Vietnam War

The Claremont Graduate school faculty were largely conservative. The Government (political science) department chair was a speechwriter for Governor Ronald Reagan. He served as my PhD dissertation chair. But his politics never got in my way. I was able to do my own intellectual work without any fear of retaliation. I felt free to pursue my interest in Marxist theory. One of the first graduate seminar papers I wrote was on the "Political Thought of Vladimir Lenin", the 1917 Russian revolutionary. My dissertation chair taught the seminar. He made clear in his remarks when grading my paper that he did not agree with what I wrote. But he gave me an "A" grade because he stated that I did an excellent scholarly job. The largely conservative graduate students of the seminar were shocked that I had elected to write about a Communist revolutionary.

In other seminars I enjoyed learning about the political philosophies of Socrates, Plato, and other Greek thinkers. Another reason I had chosen to attend Claremont was that it was considered the "Oxford" of the US at that time, meaning that graduate students were given complete independence to choose their own research interests.

I decided to take advantage of the research independence I had and chose a topic most relevant to my people. I had studied the impact of colonization on my indigenous ancestors in Mexico. I came across a book done by a Mexican sociologist by the name of Pablo Casanova that focused on what he called the "internal colonization" of the indigenous people in Mexico. I applied that framework to the experience of Mexicans in the United States after the end of the U.S. Mexican War of 1846-48 that resulted in the loss of half of the Mexican nation's territory. The experience of people living in the former Mexican territory was shaped by the same racism faced by African Americans. Specifically Mexican Americans were defined as a racially inferior people. A system of racial segregation existing in the Southern states became the same reality throughout the new states of what became the U.S. Southwest. I decided that a chapter of my doctoral dissertation would be on the topic of the Barrio as an internal colony. I later published the chapter in co-authorship with Mario Barrera and Charles Ornelas.

The Cal State LA graduate courses that I had completed for the M.A. degree were approved as part of my courses for my PhD curriculum. So I completed PhD course work within a year's time in June of 1970. It was about the same time that the California State Appellate Court decided that I, and the other 12

Chicano civil rights activists, indicted on the charges of conspiracy in 1968, were innocent based on the 1st amendment of the U.S. Constitution. I then went on the job market.

At that time, there were very few Mexican Americans with PhDs or in the process of obtaining one, so plenty of job options were available to me. I decided to apply for a faculty appointment at the UC San Diego campus because a noted Marxist scholar by the name of Herbert Marcuse was teaching there and one of his students was Angela Davis. Most importantly, Mexican American and African American students had engaged in the struggle for the creation of a Third World College that included Chicano and Black Studies. Carlos Blanco, a noted Leftist Spanish professor of Spanish literature, was a faculty supporter of the student struggle for the Third World College. He had been a participant in the Santa Barbara Conference, and we became good friends and colleagues. He was deeply committed to the development of Chicano Studies.

UC San Diego was the newest UC campus. At the time of my visit to that campus, a political science department had not yet been created, so I had to interview with faculty in the sociology department. Unfortunately, most were very conservative, and I was not hired. They were of the opinion that my theory of internal colonialism was not a legitimate academic framework.

I then was contacted by Richard Alatorre, who had been a classmate of mine at CSULA. He urged me to apply for a faculty appointment in a new Program on Comparative Cultures at the University of California, Irvine. At that time, he was a part time member of that program. He told me his heart was in electoral politics, not in pursuing an academic career. He went on to become one of the first powerful Mexican American politicians in the California State Assembly.

I was hired at UC Irvine as a Lecturer with a salary of $10,000 because I had not yet completed my PhD dissertation. Upon completion my job title would be changed to Assistant Professor with a higher salary. During my first year there, I decided that I would do what I could to open the doors to more Mexican American graduate students in the political science profession. I joined the American Political Science Association (APSA) and I organized and chaired a Chicano Caucus consisting of three other young colleagues; a recent PhD, Mario Barrera was teaching at UC Riverside, Raymond Rocco, a graduate student at UCLA, and Charles Ornelas taught at UC Santa Barbara. We decided that we would hold a panel at the 1970 APSA annual meeting held in Los Angeles, California. I chaired the panel and gave it the title of "Internal Colonialism and the Mexican American People". I invited Jesus Chavarria, a historian at UC Santa Barbara and Esteban Torres, a community activist and founder of the "East Los Angeles Community Union or TELACU, who later became a U.S. Congressman, to be on the panel. Chavarria and Torres were very knowledgeable about the colonization of Latin American countries. The former as a scholar and expert of Peru, and Torres as a one who spent much time throughout Latin America organizing trade unionists. I asked both of them to discuss the impact of colonization on oppression in those societies that they witnessed and compare it to the impact of internal colonization on Mexicans in the Southwest.

The panel established our Chicano presence in the APSA.

We also decided to place two candidates in the running for office in the APSA. I ran for the office of APSA vice president, and we asked Ralph Guzman, one of my faculty mentors at Cal State L.A. to run for the APSA Executive Council. Neither one of us got elected, but we were able to convince the APSA leadership to establish a permanent "Committee on the Status of Mexican Americans in the Discipline" that allowed us to promote efforts to recruit Mexican American graduate students at institutions of higher education throughout the nation. We requested that Ralph Guzman, by then a political science professor at UCLA, be named to chair the committee. The other members included Mario Barrera, F. Chris Garcia, Jose Angel Gutierrez, Charles Cotrell and me.

I also joined the radical Caucus for a New Political Science (CNPS) because I was in agreement with their critique of the dominant paradigms of the political science discipline that promoted the myth of the United States as a Democracy. The majority of the CNPS were white radicals; some of them had been members of the Students for Democratic Society (SDS) when they were undergraduates. The SDS had played a significant role in the organizing of the Anti-Vietnam War Movement.

I urged other Mexican American friends of mine who were graduate students in Sociology, Anthropology, and History, to organize Chicano caucuses in those professions. Jose Cuellar organized one in the Anthropology Association, Jaime Sena Rivera in the Sociology Association, and Oscar Martinez in the History Association. Our goal was to collectively contribute to opening the doors for Mexican Americans in the social sciences. My hope was that eventually that would materialize in a pool of activist scholars committed to the Chicano Movement and the establishment of Chicano Studies throughout the nation.

The writings of Italian Communist Antonio Gramsci, especially his "Prison Notebooks" had had a profound impact on my political and intellectual development. Especially his concept of organic intellectuals. I therefore wanted to contribute to the making of organic intellectuals who would be connected to the struggles for social justice being waged by Mexican Americans and other Latinos.

At the 1972 meeting of the Southwest Social Science Association, a small group of Mexican American graduate students headed by Jose Cuellar decided to form a Chicano social science association. I was not able to attend that meeting, but Jose phoned me to ask for my participation as the Chair of the APSA Chicano Caucus. I, of course, happily agreed to be part of it.

Our first meeting was held at the Highlands University in northern New Mexico, not far from Tierra Amarilla where Reies López Tijerina headed the Allianza de Pueblos Unidos engaged in the struggle to recover the Mexican lands stolen by the U.S. Empire after the U.S. Mexico War of 1846-48. Guillermo Lux, a member of the faculty arranged for us to get space on that campus where we could hold our meeting.

There were 50 Chicana and Chicano participants at the meeting from institutions throughout the nation, but most were from California. The majority were male graduate students. We engaged in a dialogue of ideas to visualize what kind of Chicano Social Science Association we wanted. We all agreed it had to be different from the traditional social science associations that we were part of. Primarily that it would be an association that would produce the research needed for the liberation of Mexican Americans from the oppressive institutions of the dominant culture and society.

We decided to name a 5-member committee that would implement the ideas discussed at the meeting. I was elected to be the chair of the committee. At that meeting, the committee decided to name our new Association, the National Association of Chicano Social Scientists (NACSS). The second decision was that I would organize the first annual meeting of NACSS at my Irvine campus. I asked Daniel Moreno, one of my graduate students, to help me. He did most of the important leg work for the conference. He became a colleague after completion of his PhD and dedicated many years to the development of our Association.

The NACSS organization underwent several name changes to incorporate scholars in the humanities, which also suffered from under-representation of Mexican American scholars. The first name change was in 1976 at our annual meeting that was held at the University of California, Berkeley. We changed the name to the National Association of Chicano Social Scientists (NACS). Soon thereafter as a direct consequence of valid Chicana feminist criticism, the next name change went from NACS to the National Association to Chicano and Chicana Studies (NACCS) to make clear the important role played by women in the development of the Association.

The Association became central to the development of Chicana/o Studies in higher education. But regretfully, it did not make Chicana/o Studies a reality in K-12 public schooling in spite of the increasing presence of Chicana and Chicano public-school teachers and Administrators. After 50 years since the 1968 student walkouts, an overall Ethnic Studies curriculum had not emerged in public education. In California, "liberal" Democratic governor Jerry Brown vetoed legislation for Ethnic Studies that was authored by Chicano/a members of the State Legislature in 2005. The Bill was introduced by Assemblyman Luis Alejo who had been one of my undergraduate students at UC Berkeley and a leader of MECha.

I take pride in having played a significant role in the making of NACCS. It has made possible the emergence of a vibrant Chicana/o Studies scholarship throughout the institutions of higher education throughout the United States.

The highlight of my time on the faculty of UC Irvine was the holding of the first NACCS conference on that campus in 1972. It was the kickoff of one of the most important developments in the intellectual history of Mexican Americans in the U.S. After that conference I went on sabbatical leave in 1974 to interview key members of La Raza Unida Party & Chicano/a Movement leaders in Texas, Colorado, and Arizona for my book on the Chicano Movement.

When I returned to resume my teaching in the Comparative Culture Program at UC Irvine, I found out that my courses on Chicano Culture had been taken off the curriculum and were no longer to be offered. The Chair of the Program, Joe Jorgensen, informed me the courses were cut because two Marxist Latino colleagues, Raul Fernandez and Gilbert Gonzales, had argued that my courses did not include a class analysis of the Latino experience. Gonzales had been a good friend who helped me develop Chicano Studies at CSULA and whom I had highly recommended to join our faculty at UC Irvine. I felt deeply betrayed by him.

My response was that if my courses were not put back on the class schedule, it represented a clear-cut issue of academic freedom. Jorgensen put my courses back on the class schedule. Regretfully, I was up for tenure and although I could not prove it, the issue contributed to the decision of the Academic Senate Committee on tenure to issue a 3-3 tie vote. The student member of the committee did not show up to cast his/her vote. It was ironic given the fact that I had been a strong supporter of students getting a vote in faculty academic senate committees.

On a tie vote UC Chancellors could make the tenure decision but the UC Irvine Chancellor told me he could not do it because the UC Regents only allowed a limited number of times for Chancellors to break the tie. And he had used up all his "tiebreaker votes". The consequence was that I was denied tenure. I decided that I had to resign from the UC Irvine faculty and move on.

Another factor was that I was undergoing a second divorce. I had remarried and it did not work out. The marriage produced my wonderful son Genaro. His mother decided to keep him although I tried to convince her to let me have him.

I had two job offers to consider for my next teaching appointments. One was with the political science department at the University of Washington in Seattle. The other one was in the Department of Ethnic Studies at UC Berkeley. I decided to apply to both. I had never planned to apply for a job in a traditional political science department, but the one at the

University of Washington appealed to me because several of the colleagues there were members of the Caucus for a New Political Science who had a Leftist political perspective. What I did not know was that there was an intense division and conflict between the Leftists and conservative traditional political scientists in that department.

After I interviewed for the job, I got a phone call from a reporter from the Seattle Times who told me that students took over the Administration building and ransacked classrooms after the Department Chair, Richard E. Flathman vetoed the vote of the department faculty to grant me a tenured appointment. Interestingly Flathman had been a member of the radical SDS during his student days. After he received his PhD, he became known for his work on the philosopher Thomas Hobbes. He was very friendly toward me when we met at the time, I visited the University of Washington campus for the interview. But his expertise on Hobbes did not help him understand my theoretical framework of Internal Colonialism.

When the reporter asked me what I thought about the student protest on the University of Washington campus after Flathman vetoed my faculty appointment my response was "oh my God, I did not know."

The MECha student organization at the University of Washington filed a request to the U.S. Department of Labor for an investigation of my case. It took 3 years before the investigation was completed. The conclusion was that indeed I had been a victim of ethnic/racial bias on the part of the Department Chair. I wanted to sue the University of Washington and called the Mexican American Legal Defense (MALDEF) organization.

Unfortunately, I was told that since the Department of Labor decision had taken 3 years, a lawsuit could not be filed because it was past the statute of limitations.

The MEChA students contacted me to find out if I still wanted the job. I had taken the job at Berkeley, and I told them I did not. I recommended that instead of demanding I be hired they should demand the hiring of other Chicano and Chicana faculty in political science and other departments. I was later informed that 5 faculty had been hired in other departments of the University. I was pleased that my case had contributed to a positive conclusion to the efforts by students to get other Mexican American faculty hired.

I have always considered negative decisions affecting me as blessings in disguise. In this case, one blessing was that I was hired at UC Berkeley to take over the Chicano Studies Program as their new chair and help build the Third World College demanded by students in their 1969 Third World Strike.

I arrived there in the Spring of 1976 as a single parent of my two oldest children from my first marriage, Carlitos and Marina. They were 9 and 10 years old respectively. Apart from facing a challenging transition as a single parent from the Irvine to the Berkeley campus, I had the challenge of taking over leadership of a Chicano Studies Program mired in internal differences with a largely graduate student part time faculty. In addition, the Asian American Studies Program was also experiencing internal ideological differences. I arrived without knowledge of those internal difficulties and specifically, of the fact that the African American Studies program had been taken out of Ethnic Studies by the Chancellor in order to fire all the radical Black faculty. He made African American Studies an independent department so he could control it and hire mainstream Black faculty.

How is it possible for us to build a Third World College without the Black Studies department I asked? The answer obviously was not possible. I joined Ron Takaki, the Department Chair and Asian American Studies coordinator and Terry Wilson, the Native American Studies coordinator in discussions that led us to conclude the best we could do was to develop a comparative Ethnic Studies curriculum. My experience teaching in the UC Irvine Comparative Cultures program was helpful. Each one of us created a course that would spearhead additional comparative courses by other faculty in our programs. At that time, outside of the UC Irvine program, no other Ethnic Studies programs or departments in the nation had a comparative Ethnic Studies curriculum. We became the first department to accomplish that feat.

I entitled my Ethnic Studies course "Comparative Protest Movements in the U.S." The course focused on the Black, Chicano/a, Asian, and Native American civil rights movements. Those were the movements that led to the creation of Ethnic Studies in higher education. The African American civil rights movement was the only one that was visible and well known at that the time due primarily to the leadership of Dr. Martin Luther King, Jr. and the courageous struggle of the African American women and men in the South that took on the white supremacy social order in that part of the country and later throughout the United States. That movement gave rise to the other movements I covered in my course.

I found the Berkeley campus to be another world. A lovely campus in the midst of what seemed to me like a forest. As the flagship of the UC system, it was much bigger and of course, much older than Irvine, one of the newer campuses in the UC system. Irvine only had one relatively high building, it was about 7 floors and was called the Humanities building. I remember coming to campus and finding what I thought was a student protest in front of the building. I went to my office to be on time for a student appointment and opened the curtains to find an ape face looking at me. Surprised, I looked out the window and saw cameras and folks that turned out to be actors. Several were wearing ape looking masks. I found out they were shooting one of the "Planet of the Apes" movies. After that incident I referred to Irvine as the "planet of the apes" campus.

The Berkeley campus in contrast was like a city within a city. Numerous buildings and parking lots. And thousands of students, faculty and staff. But faculty, students, and staff of color, were not visible. The handful of faculty of color were largely located in the African American and Ethnic Studies departments. There were only 2 Mexican American faculty in other departments.

My department colleagues selected me to represent the department in the curriculum committee of the Academic Senate where I could fight for approval of our courses. At my first meeting, a white male colleague (they were all white males) on the committee asked me if I was faculty in the Spanish department. I answered that Spanish was my worst class as an undergraduate and that my PhD was in political science. Another question asked me which country I was from. My answer was "this one". I went on to tell the committee that my ancestors were here long before any of theirs arrived here. They looked at each other and never asked me any more questions.

Another incident I'll never forget was when I parked in the faculty lot behind the Dwinelle Hall building where I taught a class. I got out of my car and a white woman asked me to move her car next. I told her that I didn't have time because I had to give a lecture. She looked at me with her mouth open. I assumed she never had met or seen a Mexican professor. The only Mexicans on campus she probably saw were gardeners, maintenance people, or those who worked in campus restaurants as dishwashers or cooks.

When I first met the handful of Mexican and other Latino/a students in my classes, they asked me if I had a PhD. They were surprised when I told them I did, but that they did not have to call me "Dr. Muñoz". They could simply call me "Profe". They had never met a professor that looked like them or especially one who grew up in barrios in El Paso and Los Angeles who shared their poor working-class background.

The internal differences amongst my program faculty did not preclude receiving respect from most of them. In particular those who became good friends were Tomas Almaguer, who went on to finish his PhD in the Sociology department, Larry Trujillo who completed his PhD in Criminology, and Francisco Hernandez who completed his EDD in the School of Education. I started recruiting for a PhD faculty for the program. The first one was Mario Barrera.

I met an intelligent and lovely student by the name of Graciela Rios whom everyone knew as Chela. She worked in the department library. She never became my student, but we became friends. I did not know it at the time we met, but she turned out to be the best blessing I found in Berkeley. I had decided to devote my life to my two children, as a single parent and not marry again. But we eventually fell in love. She went off to study abroad at the National University in Mexico City, and I would fly to visit her once a month. After her return to Berkeley, we decided to get married. We eventually had two children of our own. We named them Daniel and Marcelo.

Chela became a wonderful stepmother to my children AND a wonderful mother to our own children and eventually a wonderful grandmother to our four grandchildren, Emany, Amaya, Quezali, and Marcelito Calixto. Without Chela it would have been difficult to survive the rigors of academic and the political struggles on the Berkeley campus and in the community. She became my confidant and the backbone of our marriage. She also became a comrade in the struggle for social justice. She served as a medical social worker in the community trenches of struggle for survival waged by poor people and especially Latino immigrant families and their medically fragile children.

Chapter 6

Conclusion

Photo left: 1978. Speaking in protest of the US Supreme Court Bakke ruling, a major setback for affirmative action college admissions. Photo right: 2003. Participating in anti-Iraq war protest in San Francisco. *(Photo credits: author's archives)*

During all my years of college and university teaching, from 1968 until my retirement from the University of California, Berkeley, I was also an activist. My activism started when, as an undergraduate student and Vietnam War-era veteran, I participated in the first mass anti–Vietnam War protest held in Los Angeles in 1965. I continued to march in many other antiwar protest actions until the war finally ended.

During that time, I also participated in demonstrations in support of the United Farm Workers Movement led by César Chávez and Dolores Huerta, and in support of the Southern civil rights movement led by Dr. Martin Luther King, Jr. I connected with leaders of that movement's Student Non-Violent Coordinating Committee (SNCC) when I met Stokely Carmichael when he was working closely with Dr. King. After the 1968 Chicano student walkouts in East Los Angeles, I became one of the leaders of the emerging Chicano civil rights movement that was sparked by those walkouts.

I also became involved with other movements that were fighting for the nonviolent revolution that Dr. King had called for. My military experience in Korea during Gen. Park's right-wing coup in that country led me to research the role of U.S. imperialism in Asia, Latin America and elsewhere in the Third World. And after I was imprisoned in 1968 for my role as one of the organizers of the East Los Angeles student walkouts, I became convinced that my country was not a true democracy. I remembered the quote "Something is rotten in the state of Denmark" from Shakespeare's *Hamlet,* and I was convinced that something was also rotten in the USA. Many others felt the same way, and I was invited by members of the Communist Party, the Socialist Workers Party, and the newer communist organizations that emerged in the late 1960s to join their parties. Two of those newer ones were the Line of March, which was founded by a diverse group of youth of color, and the Chicano

August 29th Movement. However, I did not find the hardcore Marxist ideological bent of those organizations to my liking.

I met Dorothy Healy after she resigned as chair of the California Communist Party. She invited me to join a new Left organization she had helped found called the New American Movement (NAM). This new organization was to be free of the CP's outdated Marxist ideology; she envisioned it as a nonsectarian socialist organization. After attending one of those meetings, it became clear to me that it would take a lot of my energy and time to help develop that new organization, and I therefore decided to concentrate on studying for my PhD and engaging in the research on communist and socialist political thought.

I continued, however, to play a leadership role in the Chicano civil rights movement, in the La Raza Unida party (LRUP), which emerged from the movement. I was committed to contributing to the development of the LRUP as an independent party free of what I called the two-party dictatorship of the Democratic and Republican Parties. In this work I came to know Rodolfo "Corky" Gonzales and José Ángel Gutierrez, who emerged as the two key leaders of the party. Corky was a former championship-caliber boxer who became a bail bonds businessman and later a founder of the Crusade for Justice organization based in Denver; he co-founded that organization as a direct result of the lack of support to run for mayor of Denver. He was told by the white leadership of the Democratic Party that "Mexicans don't become mayor of the city." José Ángel was a student activist who co-founded the La Raza Unida Party in South Texas after being a leader of the Mexican American Youth Organization (MAYO) in San Antonio. We both had been political science graduate students and had become friends when he joined the American Political Science Association's APSA's Chicano Caucus, which I had co-founded and chaired. We later served as members of the Committee on the Status of Mexican Americans in the Profession

Unfortunately, ideological divisions developed between José Ángel and Corky and their respective constituents. At the first (and unfortunately the last) national convention of the party in 1972, which was held in my hometown of El Paso, I argued for party unity. I wrote a position paper arguing that the party should be open to both cultural nationalist and revolutionary nationalist ideologies. I identified the former as the framework of José Ángel and his followers, and the latter as the ideological framework of Corky and his followers. Both groups reflected a focus on Chicano identity, but José Ángel's group focused on electoral politics and Corky's group focused on providing a political education in the barrios calling for the emergence of revolutionary alternatives to the status quo. In my paper I held both perspectives to be legitimate frameworks within the context of La Raza Unida Party. Both these ideological frameworks focused on racial oppression, but the revolutionary nationalist framework focused on both race and class in the context of socialism. Unfortunately, at this time patriarchy was not on the agenda and did not emerge as an issue for the party until later, when Chicana feminists emerged in the party leadership.

The 1972 LRUP convention included an election for the party leadership: Corky and José Ángel were the leading candidates. Reies Lopez Tijerina, the leader of the land grants movement in New Mexico, was a third candidate. José Ángel was victorious and took over the leadership of the party. After the election, I bumped into Corky in the hotel elevator, and he complained to me that the "intellectuals" won the vote for the party leadership. Although he did not specify who he meant by "intellectuals," I assumed that his talk about "intellectuals" reflected the fact that José Ángel and I had become university professors. He also told me that he believed that José Ángel won because most of the delegates, though from throughout the U.S., were originally from Texas and had migrated to other states seeking work. I agreed it was true. The ideological split contributed to the decline of the party. By 1974, La Raza Unida had won only a few local elections in South Texas but had largely disappeared throughout the rest of the Southwest.

After its decline I dropped out of the party and decided to participate in political work that would foster multiracial unity in the U.S. Left. Based on my participation in the Chicano Movement and the LRUP, I concluded that ethnic nationalism, either cultural or revolutionary, had serious limitations, and that neither ideological approach would result in a viable path toward liberation of Mexican Americans and other people of color from racism or class and gender oppression When I joined the faculty at UC Irvine in 1970 I had become a member of a multiracial Left collective mostly white and Latino, which founded a journal we called Latin American Perspectives on Capitalism and Socialism. We were a combination of faculty and graduate students in the Southern California area who represented diverse Left ideologies. I also became active in a grassroots Left committee called the Los Angeles Solidarity Committee for Latin American Revolution. This group was formed in response to the assassination of Salvador Allende, Chile's president, and contributed to opposition to the U.S.-supported Pinochet dictatorship that emerged after the Allende assassination and the imprisonment, torture, and killing of thousands of Allende's supporters.

After joining the faculty at UC Berkeley in 1976, I became a founding member of the West Coast branch of the Socialist Committees of Correspondence. Angela Davis and Leon Wofsy were two friends of mine who also joined; both of them had been members of the Communist Party. Angela had also been active in the Black Panther Party and had been imprisoned on a trumped-up charge of murder. After she was freed from prison, she completed her PhD and became a UC colleague of mine when she joined the faculty at UC Santa Cruz.

Leon Wofsy was a colleague of mine at my UC Berkeley campus, where he was a scientist in the Microbiology Department. He was the son of a CP leader back in the 1930s, and like his father, he became a leader of the party and served as the chair of the CP Labor Youth League. We worked closely together on the Faculty for Peace Committee and the Committee for Human Rights in El Salvador and Central America, and the Faculty Against Apartheid in South Africa. He passed away in 2019 at the age of ninety-eight.

In response to U.S. intervention in civil wars in El Salvador and Nicaragua Leon and I became members of the Faculty for Human Rights in El Salvador and Central America (FACHRES). We worked closely with community organizations in the Bay Area that supported the movements against the rightwing terror in those countries. For example, we organized delegations of distinguished progressive faculty at universities throughout the U.S. who had received Nobel Prizes. We sent those delegations to El Salvador to negotiate the release of students and faculty who had been tortured and imprisoned for opposing the U.S.-supported government.

Along with Angela Davis, Leon and I also became members of the Faculty Against Apartheid in South Africa. We marched in support of the anti-apartheid movement led by Nelson Mandela, and along with other UC Berkeley faculty and local African American community leaders. We demanded that the University of California system end its investments in companies active in Apartheid South Africa. Some of us were arrested when we protested at the offices of the president of the University of California. Our protest efforts paid off and the Regents of the University voted to divest from companies that supported the Apartheid government.

In 1986, I became a founding member of the Rainbow Coalition led by Jesse Jackson. Although I remained critical of the U.S. two-party dictatorship, I became part of the Jesse Jackson presidential campaign as a Democrat in 1988., serving as an organizer and an adviser on immigration issues. I saw Jackson's campaign as an important step toward the formation of a multiracial mass Left movement. The campaign to make Jesse Jackson the first major African American Democratic Party candidate faced many obstacles, including lack of support from within the party structure and lack of sufficient funds to pay for media advertising. He still received millions of votes. Another obstacle was that many U.S. Democratic voters were not yet ready for a Black president. For example, I will never forget when a white liberal colleague who was a distinguished historian told me that he liked Jackson, but did not like it when Jackson spoke, "He sounded too Black."

After that election I became active in the San Francisco Bay Area in various protest actions against U.S. imperialism around the world. In addition, I joined the Movement for Jobs, Peace and Justice. Later my friend Betita Martinez, one of the leading Chicana feminists in the country, who had been active in the 1960s Student Nonviolent Coordinating Committee, invited me to join her in the founding of the Center for Multiracial Justice based in San Francisco. Other founders included Manning Marable, an activist who became a prominent Black scholar, and Angela Davis.

With my wife Graciela "Chela" Rios Muñoz, I also had the pleasure of becoming a founder in 1995 of a Berkeley grassroots organization we called Latino/as for Justice and another grassroots organization in Albany, California, Albany Families for Multicultural Education. I have remained a member of the National Immigrant and Refugee Rights organization (NIRR) and the Veterans for Peace.

In the years since 1968 it has not been easy to pursue a course as a nonviolent revolutionary. I have learned many lessons in the struggle to make the nonviolent "revolution of values" that Dr. Martin Luther King, Jr. called for. I learned an important first lesson as a leader of the Chicano movement. That lesson was that mass protest by itself is not enough to fundamentally change the structure of power responsible for the oppression of people of color in our society. It does not end the oppression of the poor and women, especially women of color or the discrimination against LGBT people. The state apparatus does not end its repressive work when faced by mass protest, although it may reluctantly agree to some reforms. The system of injustice continues. It does not matter whether the president is a Republican or Democrat. For example, President Trump not only supported those institutions, but also gave legitimacy to white supremacy advocates. When Joe Biden became president, he continued supporting those institutions although he did not support white supremacy groups. The Department of Homeland Security's ICE unit continues to criminalize, terrorize, and imprison undocumented workers and their families. The U.S. Congress terminated the FBI's 1960s Counter-Intelligence Program, known as COINTELPRO. But the FBI continues to engage in the surveillance of American citizens opposed to U.S. government policies that sustain the power of corporations and super-rich white men at the expense of human rights.

All the various other movements I have been a part of collectively produced reforms in the United States that have been important for the oppressed in our society. But they have not been able to make fundamental structural changes to radically transform our society into an authentic multiracial democracy.

Today, we once again find ourselves in critical and challenging times—in some ways the worst of times. I never thought that after over fifty years of participation in the struggle we would be living the nightmare our society is now experiencing.

The 2020 presidential election victory by Biden and Kamala Harris did rid us of the Trump presidency influence. That was a cause for celebration. But the power structure has not changed. The two-party dictatorship will continue and the capitalist corporate structure that finances it will remain the same. The war-based foreign policy of the U.S. empire will continue, and its 800 military bases worldwide will not be closed down. In addition, the Biden administration continues to support the state of Israel in its oppression of the Palestinian people, and it will continue its anti-Cuba policies, such as the U.S. blockade that undermines Cuba's foreign trade to secure food supplies and medical equipment.

The new Biden administration reflects more diversity, but the reality of racial, ethnic, patriarchal, and LGBT injustice will continue. The violent white nationalist organizations that Trump nurtured and supported will not disappear. The millions of those who voted for Trump won't either. The vast majority, although not necessarily adhering to white nationalism, will remain loyal Republican Party members and most of those will continue to support rightwing politics.

I feel it imperative that progressives and revolutionaries continue to speak truth to power and to join those of diverse ideological points of view in protest actions against the U.S. government and others responsible for foreign and domestic policies that cause social, economic, and environmental injustice.

The silence against the wars that continue in the Middle East and elsewhere will not be broken. We must give rise to a mass movement that will openly criticize our government and hold it accountable for continuing a war-based foreign policy. Those of us, especially veterans, who favor the immediate withdrawal of our troops, must demand it because we do support them, and we want them home safe and out of harm's way.

We have lost enough of our young men and women of all races and ethnicities on the battlefields. Those who have survived combat have returned home with PTSD and other emotional problems. We must also speak out against the killing of any more innocent people in those countries. Finally, we must demand that all the 800 U.S. military bases around the world be closed.

We must demand that the trillion dollars that has been spent on war and military assistance be diverted to fight poverty at home, improve the public schools, and support social welfare institutions and programs. Today, over 35 million Americans live in poverty, and African Americans and Latina and Latino are overrepresented in those poverty rates.

We must demand that the U.S. Congress stop supporting the bailout of the corporate, banking, and financial institutions responsible for economic crises, and that instead they must bail out the poor and the working underclass.

On the home front, we must demand that the police war against Black and Brown people be stopped—in particular, the police must stop murdering unarmed Black and Brown young men and women.

The war against Latino/a undocumented immigrants must also be stopped. They are forced to work as a cheap labor force, and they are therefore most vulnerable to economic and social injustice. They are treated by the government as criminals, although they are innocent victims of what I call a government terrorist war led by the ICE, the enforcement immigration agency of the Department of Homeland Security. ICE military-style raids have taken place at the workplace and at the homes of undocumented workers' families. Further, the U.S. Congress must demilitarize the U.S–Mexico border. We must demand that the president and Congress produce a comprehensive immigration policy based on the human rights of undocumented workers and their families.

Prior to his assassination in 1968, Dr. King called for the nation to dedicate itself to a nonviolent War on Poverty. He had decided to build a multiracial coalition of all poor people, inclusive of white, Black, Indigenous, Latino/a, and Asian. As part of the building process, he had started organizing a Poor People's March on Washington. Dr. King believed that the time had come to transform civil rights struggles into a mass movement for human rights because war and poverty negatively impacts all the American poor regardless of race and ethnicity.

We must do the same today and build multiracial poor people's coalitions, inclusive of the immigrant poor, both documented and undocumented, throughout our nation. And hopefully, those coalitions can lead toward the organizing of another march on Washington to demand that the President and the Congress declare a permanent war on poverty that would last until poverty is eliminated.

Dr. King did not hesitate to speak truth to power, no matter the consequences. We must do the same today. We must use his legacy as the inspiration for us to be active citizens beyond election campaign season, and we must do so in our communities, in our workplaces, and elsewhere. We must become community organizers and continue to carry the torch for hope and for fundamental, not symbolic, change. Dr. King's ideas remain vibrant to those of us committed to social justice, human rights, and peace. The words he wrote and spoke on the issues of his time remain meaningful for us today. We must put them into practice and keep his revolutionary spirit alive and struggle to build an authentic multiracial democracy committed to social justice and peace at home and abroad. Dr. King's work has inspired me to have my own dream for an authentic revolutionary multiracial democracy:

I have a dream that Americans of all colors, ethnicities, cultures, religions, sexual preferences, the able and disabled, men and women, will give birth to an authentic multiracial democracy.

A democracy that will promote and nurture racial and ethnic diversity and equality beyond symbolic tokenism.

A democracy that will promote social, economic, and environmental justice, religious tolerance, and peace at home and abroad.

A democracy with a government that will include representation of every diverse group at the table of political power on behalf of the people, not the military-corporate-prison complex.

A democracy with a national multi-party electoral system where candidates for office include the poor and working class, not just those who are rich or middle class. An electoral system where every vote will in fact be counted and not discarded in favor of influence by corporate lobbyists.

A democracy where human needs are prioritized and not the needs of the rich and the corporations, with a government bureaucracy that assures the safety of our citizens, especially the poor, when natural disasters take place. No more Katrinas!

A democracy that honors all workers, those who are citizens and those who are not, the documented and the undocumented.

A democracy that defines health care, housing, childcare, and education as human rights.

A democracy that prioritizes youth as the most important investment for the future of our nation and builds more schools instead of more prisons.

A democracy that wages war against poverty and not against sovereign nations that do not represent a direct threat to our security.

A democracy that does not support dictatorships throughout the world.

A democracy that will be based on love and compassion and not hate and greed.

In conclusion, I have learned that struggle is life and life is struggle—but most importantly, that victory is in the struggle!

Author Biography

At the Angel de la Independencia monument in Mexico City, June 2012. Author signing a poster in support of the "Yo Soy 132" protest movement—a democratic movement against state violence and repression in Mexico. (*Photo credit: Graciela Eulalia Rios Muñoz*)

Dr. Carlos Muñoz, Jr. was born in the "Segundo barrio" in El Paso, Texas, and raised in the barrios of East Los Angeles, California. He is the son of poor working-class Mexican immigrants. He earned his AA from Los Angeles City Community College, his BA with honors in Political Science from California State University at Los Angeles and his PhD in Government from the Claremont Graduate University. He is Professor Emeritus in the Department of Ethnic Studies and

Adjunct Faculty, Center for Latin American Studies, University of California, Berkeley. After 47 years of teaching in higher education, he has gained international prominence as political scientist, historian, journalist, and public intellectual. His book, *Youth, Identity, Power: The Chicano Movement,* won the Gustavus Myers Book Award for "outstanding scholarship in the study of the Chicano movement and human rights in the United States".

www.ingramcontent.com/pod-product-compliance
Lightning Source LLC
LaVergne TN
LVHW041642060526
838200LV00040B/1682